# THE
# ELDEST
# DAUGHTER
# EFFECT

How Firstborn Women —
like Oprah Winfrey, Sheryl Sandberg,
JK Rowling and Beyoncé
— Harness their Strengths

# THE
# ELDEST
## DAUGHTER
## EFFECT

How Firstborn Women —
like Oprah Winfrey, Sheryl Sandberg,
JK Rowling and Beyoncé
— Harness their Strengths

## Lisette Schuitemaker & Wies Enthoven

FINDHORN PRESS

Findhorn Press
One Park Street
Rochester, Vermont 05767
www.findhornpress.com

Findhorn Press is a division of Inner Traditions International

ISBN 978-1-84409-707-4

Cataloging-in-Publication Data for this title is available from the British Library

Printed and bound in the United States

Translation by Lisette Schuitemaker
Edited by Jacqui Lewis
Cover design by Richard Crookes
Text design and layout by Damian Keenan

Authors photos by Eveline Renaud (p. 192 & cover)

# Contents

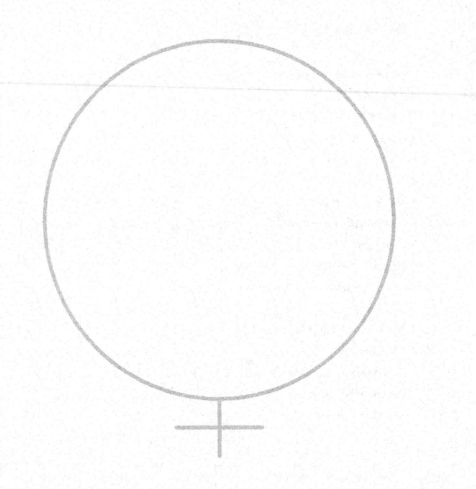

# Introduction

We struck up a friendship over thirty years ago. With Lisette quite tall and Wies quite small, with Wies being a mother of two and Lisette a mere aunt, we look very different and have shaped our lives differently. Yet, time and again we've come to the conclusion that the two of us are remarkably similar.

We're both eldest daughters. That this position within our families has shaped us both to a large degree has been a stunning discovery. Since we began to look at our similarities through the eldest-daughter lens, we have become aware of underlying patterns in our lives that we share with millions of other eldest daughters in the world. Thus the idea arose to dive into our particular birth order position and write a book together on the effect of this specific position within the family. Although there is growing interest in the lifelong effects of your place in the family, as far as we know, this is a first: a book for eldest daughters by eldest daughters.

We boldly state that eldest daughters resemble one another. That we are alike in so many aspects that we resemble each other more than we do our own siblings. Of course, in many ways we are each different and unique, but still we dare say that eldest daughters are one of a kind.

With this book we want to celebrate our birth position and show how wonderfully close we eldest daughters are to one another. We aim to shed light on the patterns that we share in our thinking, feeling and doing. These patterns run deep as they stem from the period when we were the only child; with our parents admiring our every move, many of us have felt like a little queen, but then, all of a sudden, a sibling was born and we fell from our throne: from one minute to the next we became the eldest.

## The Eldest Daughter Day

To start our research off we organized a day exclusively for eldest daughters. Over one hundred women of all ages attended this Eldest Daughter Day in Amsterdam, the Netherlands in March 2014. We had envisioned that women who had never met before would recognize one another as if they were at a school reunion and that is exactly what happened. As soon as they fell into animated conversations while hanging up their coats, we knew something special was afoot. In the workshops that we had designed for facts and stories to surface, they talked as if there was no tomorrow. They opened up to each other and to us, as researchers, as if we had known each other all our lives. In a way we had. In sharing what the effects on their lives had been of the role that they, as the eldest daughter, fulfilled and continued to fulfil, all of us were moved by these unexpected levels of recognition.

In the weeks and months that followed we immersed ourselves in the invaluable information that we had gathered on this one day. We followed the steps of Grounded Theory, the method also used by the professor, bestselling author and yes, eldest daughter Brené Brown. This relatively new way of working systematically with qualitative data wants you not to have a hypothesis that you go out and find evidence for, but to do exactly the opposite: you start with as much of a clean slate as possible.

The underlying idea is that the fewer assumptions and pre-stated theories you have, the more open you will be to what people are going to say about the topic of research. The method predicts that when you categorize the conversations and order your findings, you will start to see patterns. You will discover storylines that present themselves over and over again. These lines and patterns, rising out of people's daily life experiences, will be the basis of your theory. The theory that you build from the ground up can then be tested and supported with information gathered from the available literature and research by others.

So day after day we gazed at the long lists of subjects from the eldest daughters' lives that we had distilled from the stories they had shared with us. What patterns could we detect? We arranged and rearranged our material, until one day a coherent image started to present itself. Just like the method said it would. Suddenly we saw what had been staring us in the face all along: time and again we ran into five major qualities that eldest daughters all described to some degree and that siblings often named when referring to their eldest sister. Once we had these big five qualities down, the rest all started to fall into place. That is why the five major qualities that are typical for firstborn women form the core of this book.

We then went on to complement our own research with what we found in literature and online sources. We avidly combed through books by the growing number of psychologists who acknowledge the influence of birth order. We found research by academics who, sometimes begrudgingly, had concluded from their data that birth order does indeed have an effect on – for instance – intelligence. We read autobiographies of eldest daughters who had made their way in the world with the unmistakable qualities we all share. We tested what we found on ourselves, other eldest daughters, books by well-respected psychologists and all the other data that we had gathered, until we had a clear picture.

## Broad strokes

Obviously there is no one single factor that, to the exclusion of all others, drives the course of a person's life. Where you were born determines whether your staple food is bread or chapattis, pasta or rice. In which era you enter this world marks whether you wear a gown or blue jeans. Who your parents are, what they have been through in their lives, the unique combination of their genes and your character – all of this has a part to play in how you turn out. However, in psychology up until recently the influence of your particular place within your birth family has not been given the attention we feel it deserves.

Our experience is that birth order merits further research. Again and again we noticed what an eye-opener it was for eldest daughters to find out that certain qualities are not as individual as they had tended to think. An extraordinary sense of responsibility, a tendency to take the lead, a fear of making mistakes, being hit hard by criticism, and caring for others to the point of exhaustion – these are all qualities that eldest daughters typically display. Many eldest daughters grow into hands-on, caring, dutiful women because these traits were fostered in them as firstborns.

Once you begin to see the pattern in the characteristics that eldest daughters share, you may start to feel a sense of liberation. As is the case with any form of increased self-knowledge, you will find that a growing awareness of the patterns that underlie your behaviour gives you a choice. When you understand why you've always wanted to get everything right all the time, this insight can help you to better manage future occasions when your tendency towards perfectionism arises.

Now you can consciously determine your action and choose whether you wish to apply this quality or not, instead of just responding to what happens. Once you realize why it is that you always feel responsible for all and sundry, you can start to allow yourself to hold back so you are not forever the one who makes the reservations for the family dinner, buys the collective present or picks up sweet old Auntie Sue. You'll learn that it is OK if you go back on what you had implied you would do. You'll find the world does not end when you act without having gone out of your way to obtain permission from all involved.

As authors, we have benefitted greatly from the insights we have gained in researching and writing this book. There is no doubt in our minds that the more you deepen your insight into the patterns of the eldest-daughter paradigm, the freer you will start to feel. You will no longer need to be scared, as Lisette has been ever since she can remember, that people invariably expect too much and once they get to know you, they'll be disappointed and will want to get rid of you. Nor do you need to be anxious like Wies, who tended to think that all she had accomplished up to now didn't really account for much, that she needed to push herself even harder to make sure people could see who she is.

Once you see the patterns, you'll find, as we did, that people are on to us big time. In movies and books a woman only needs to be portrayed as somewhat thoughtful and astute and the message is clear: she is the eldest. In conversations with women and men during the year of our research many had a clear image of the eldest daughter: 'the dutiful one who wants to take care of everybody' was a description many gave without much prompting. 'The one who feels perpetually responsible for everyone and everything' was another one that often came up. While we like to think that each and every one of us is unique, we do also live our lives according to patterns.

## Helpful insights

We wrote this book primarily for eldest daughters. Many of those we spoke to in the course of our research have let us know how helpful the insights into the patterns we shared have been to them. 'So that is why I usually take the lead without really meaning to,' more than one of them sighed. Others said: 'People tell me that I hold myself to high standards and I've never really understood what they meant. Now I begin to see why I've always felt I have to do my utmost.' With great honesty some of them shared: 'I sometimes feel jealous of my youngest sister, who takes life so much more in her stride than I do. Now that we are both adults I can still marvel at the ease with which she talks to people, makes friends and approaches life in general. I wish I had more of her flair.'

This book is, however, not only for eldest daughters. Maybe you are not a firstborn but, after one or more boys, you are the first daughter in your family. Women with an older brother often offered the same comment: 'He doesn't do it.' They would nod at us, implying that we would surely understand what they meant. We did. We understood that yes, he had been the first to go to school and he had paved the way for them in the areas of pocket money and coming home late. Also it had certainly been an advantage to get to know boys through him; but now that their aging mother needs more care, he is nowhere to be seen. 'Functional eldest daughter' is the technical term for the younger sister, who jumps into the gap he leaves and takes responsibility. These women have not, like real eldest daughters, had to take the first step in virtually everything, but many of them still end up taking responsibility for the well-being of the family and they do this brilliantly.

Maybe you are mother to an eldest daughter and you would love to have more insight into her inner life. What is the reason that she feels, or felt, so responsible at such a young age? Why is she so thoughtful and what makes her want to drill her younger sisters or brothers in the way she thinks is right? You might have an older sister, a colleague who is the eldest, a boss, a partner or a friend who you have never fully been able to make out and who you will understand better through the patterns we describe.

## How this book is set up

We begin at the beginning; the first four chapters deal mainly with the past. We describe the time for which the eldest was the only child and the important impact of these first years alone with her parents. Then we look at when number two arrives and suddenly the only child needs to adapt to being the eldest. The conclusions we as little girls draw from that event are formative for the way we will develop ourselves from now on. You will see the pitfalls for the eldest daughter and the qualities we cultivate on the basis of the new family constellation.

In chapter five we present the five major qualities that we have found in eldest daughters. Each of us forges a unique combination of these five traits, but the same potential patterns run in all of us.

The danger of wanting to be perfect is inherent and so we gave this paralyzing predicament a chapter of its own, chapter six. In chapters seven to eleven we show how eldest daughters find their way in the world with the qualities they have developed in their youth. We shed light on the five major life areas: friendship, work, love, your own eldest daughter and your ongoing relationship with the others you grew up with.

At the back of the book you will find four of the exercises we used to conduct our research during the Eldest Daughter Day. You can do these exercises by yourself or with others. For those who want to delve deeper we have included a bibliography with short descriptions of what each book offers. Finally, you will find a test that allows you to gauge your insight into the effects and typical qualities of each place in the birth order.

Writing this book has taught us a lot and that is why we don't leave ourselves out of the equation. Each chapter begins with a glance into the life of one of us. To be honest, seeing how predictable our feelings and thoughts as eldest daughters are has at times been challenging; we don't think we're alone in wanting to be unique! However, when all is said and done, it is liberating to realize that all eldest daughters go through more or less the same experiences and draw more or less the same conclusions: 'If only I am sweet and good enough, they'll let me stay' or something along those lines. Once we acknowledge that this birth position offers a particular human experience, we can move beyond the reactive patterns and be who we truly are.

We have illustrated the text with quotes from eldest daughters of some fortune and fame, because with this book we want to encourage eldest daughters young and old. Yes, we are bossy at times, we tend to take things overly serious, we work too hard or doubt our own abilities too much, but we are also pillars of strength, faithful friends, hands-on helpers, enterprising organizers and caring colleagues, bosses, daughters and partners. Even if we ourselves may have a hard time believing it, we are women who people can count on.

# 1

# A little queen

. . .

**WIES** When I was about eight years old, I had a girlfriend who was already ten. I adored her, not least because she had an older brother. In my eyes this offered numerous advantages. For one, my friend's parents allowed her to go to the fair in the evening when it was dark, because her brother would be with her. She was kind enough to ask him if it would be all right if I tagged along. He said yes. I was over the moon. I ran to my father to announce this wonderful news. He said no. Going to the fair in the dark? That would have to wait until I was older. To his mind – and he was probably right – the fact that the two of us would be accompanied by the older brother was no guarantee of my safety whatsoever. If I had my heart set on going to the fair I could do so during the day in the company of a grown-up.

On no other occasion have I been so furious with my father. I cannot recall being in that state of agitation before or after this incident and I have never felt this rebellious again. Totally incongruently with my normal character, I sought revenge. Though I have no recollection of the action itself, I vividly remember my father's reaction when he discovered that I had taken my felt-tip pens and coloured in part of the wallpaper in the living room. He was livid.

Now, my father was a calm, friendly and kind-hearted man who gave my younger sister and me lots of leeway. I cannot recall him exploding from anger ever before, so when he did, it felt to me as if the world was coming to an end. I had done something completely out of character. I had not been my usual good and obedient self. I had gone into all-out resistance as if I were a spoilt princess denied the fulfilment of a

14

silly wish. This irked my father, because if there was anything that he disliked deeply, it was children with a pout. Sulking was not an option in our home – at least to the extent that my father could have his way; with three women in the house the occasional pout proved inevitable.

The incident with the felt-tip pens is etched in my memory. For a long time I assumed I had been so shocked because my father was hardly ever cross with us; I wasn't accustomed to outrage. Of course, his outburst had frightened me out of my wits. I always thought that was why this particular incident has stayed with me for so long – my sister generally remembers much more of our younger years, while I have forgotten a lot. Now, however, I am inclined to think that this event made such a lasting impression because I suddenly understood what happened when I did not fulfil my eldest-daughter role. I had experience of my father being annoyed with others. He could, for instance, become highly irritated with politicians with whom he disagreed or bad service in a restaurant. He just had never been angry with me before.

I now realize that I never gave him reason to be. In order to secure my place as the queen within the family I had from a young age assumed the role of the responsible and caring eldest. I saw how happy I could make my parents by behaving in this way, which in turn made me feel appreciated. It was a good arrangement for all of us. Being the eldest and the wisest was the assignment my father had given me. In general, I stuck to that, until the fateful day that I wanted to go to the fair.

## Undivided attention

In one fell swoop your birth has turned the life of your parents upside down. However many stories they have heard about having children, however many books they have read on the subject, it is just like life itself: experience is the only way you can truly find out how it is. There you are, their first child. You are a miracle to your new-minted parents, your single mother or your adoptive family. All their attention goes on you, you and nothing else. You only have to heave a little sigh and they run over to your cot. Your every smile and every movement is recorded in pictures and videos, shared and written about. As soon as you start to cry, they prick up their ears. Does she need a clean nappy? Is she hungry? Thus two super-loving adults are continually busy keeping their newborn happy.

Once you are a toddler, all their time is devoted to you. They read aloud to you a lot, build countless Lego castles, curtains are embroidered with a whole zoo, brand-new ergonomically tested highchairs bought, and the number of pictures taken of you keeps growing by the day. Every action you perform, however insignificant, is greeted with applause from those around you. Your first incomprehensible drawing, your first unintelligible words. Strangely, everyone in the family, your father, mother, grandparents, all seem to have been a witness to your first unaided step, even if they were not all sitting together at the time of this momentous event.

## Rules of your own

As the firstborn you have specific ideas about what you like and don't like and you soon learn how to communicate your preferences to all concerned. No, you would rather not lie in your cot by yourself. So you cry loudly when they leave you there and they will take you back to the living room with them. You like to drink from the blue cup and not the red one. You like green apples better than yellow ones, skirts better than trousers. For the time being your parents are willing to move heaven and earth for you. So you get accustomed to having things your way.

> 'Before Louis came into my life, I had no idea what love was. I had no idea what lack of sleep was. I had no idea what milestones felt like.'
>
> — SANDRA BULLOCK in *The Daily Mail*

From the moment of conception, your father and mother are first-timers in all they experience. This, of course, also goes for single parents. They are all embarking on something that is completely new to them. Something that will never be repeated in exactly the same way, however many children they may have together later. Now they are full of expectancy, which started long before you were born. First they kept the big secret between themselves. Gradually they divulged it to people close to them. The pregnancy is exciting, as is the delivery – and then, to top it all, there you are. You are all they could have ever imagined and at the same time there is no way in which you resemble what they had fantasized about.

The only thing they know in their bones is that they will protect you for ever. Just this question remains wide open: how are they going to go about that? All of a sudden they are not just a couple in love, each with their own names, but they have acquired an extra name: now they are 'Mummy' and 'Daddy'. Once you start to mumble your first words, they even surprise themselves by referring to each other that way. Through you they learn by doing what it takes to take care of a newborn baby. Or as the psychologist and bestselling author Dr Kevin Leman writes to his eldest daughter in the dedication of his book *The Firstborn Advantage*: 'As new, excited parents we made all the mistakes. Yes, we admit we practiced on you. You, our firstborn, were our guinea pig.'

### First love

New parents live and learn. The brand-new father and mother adore you and at the same time they are full of questions and insecurities. They have never had to deal with this sort of thing before and you don't come with an instruction manual. Did that red spot on your cheek appear overnight or did you already have it? Are you eating enough, getting enough sleep? Would it be bad if she just came into bed with us again, they ask one another. These are just practicalities. What to think of all the feelings you as their firstborn elicit? How does your mother see you? Did she have doting parents or is this her chance to give to you what she never received herself? Is your father someone who shows his emotions easily or does he shy away from physical contact and signal his love for you in other ways? Whatever your parents' styles, it all has a great impact on you. Parents tend to see themselves in their children, especially with their first child. This might even result in some squabbling over your cot when tactless mothers-in-law claim you as a spitting image of others in their family.

A first child is like a first love, say therapist Ronald and journalist Lois Richardson in their co-authored book *Birth Order & You*. So special. So unexpectedly, unreservedly fulfilling. So intense. So scary as well. Your birth made your parents into parents. All their attention in that first period goes on you and you alone. Your parents, your grandparents and other members of the family cannot get enough of you. Everything you do, learn and master is extraordinary.

The pressure on your parents to get everything right is huge. Your mother is still recuperating from her first delivery, which is no small feat in itself, and in those first weeks hormones rule; a visit to the health centre when your growth is shown to be a bit less than average might completely defeat her. Your father loves you to bits but he must also deal with the fact that your mother has eyes only for you. Those first, bumpy experiences make parenthood seem so much more complex than it had seemed in theory.

> '*The world revolves around the sun. That's odd. I thought it revolved around me.*'
>
> — LUCY VAN PELT, eldest daughter character in *Peanuts*
>
> by Charles M. Schulz

Experts in the field of family relations point out how much new parents bring to their parenting from the way they themselves were raised. As a parent, certain habits that were common in your own family may be so familiar that you don't even notice you have them. When the two halves of a couple have had very different upbringings, then obviously they will have some work to do to find a balance in their new life with you. This may express itself in decisions as simple as whether it is good for you to have the window open or closed while you sleep; whether you are to be picked up at your first little cry or be left to your own devices for a bit; whether you need a change of clothes after you've spilled your food or can toddle around with a stain on your shoulder. (The latter may go for the parents as well). Your father may secretly have dreamt of a son, even if only because gender-wise that would be more familiar to him. All of a sudden he needs to adjust the image that he had formed in his mind.

Some psychologists, mostly female ones, state that women in their heart of hearts prefer their first baby to be a girl so that they themselves are in a way reborn. 'This reflects the eternal longing for a new beginning. To be able to make a fresh start on a clean slate,' is how Dutch psychologist and author of a handbook about developmental psychology Rita Kohnstamm describes this. The fact that some pregnant women would rather their firstborn be a girl has a lot to do with what is recognizable: they know a girl's body from the inside out.

## Newborn parents

The birth is not just yours. The world acquires a newborn father and mother as well. It goes without saying that this will have an impact on their relationship. However good or unstable they are together, your arrival means a lot to both of them. Consciously or unconsciously, your mother may have certain expectations of your father as a partner, which may or may not come true. He may prove to be a much more engaged parent than her own father ever was. Not assuming that, though, she has already engaged her own mother to help her and the fresh father is disappointed when denied the opportunity to do certain tasks.

Or your mother may have firmly intended to go back to work immediately after your birth, but now that you are here, she finds she just wants to stay at home and potter around with you. How does she deal with that? How strong is the love between your parents? Do they help and support one another; can they agree on how they want to raise you? Have they assumed they had more or less the same views on life, only to find there are many issues that they now need to address? Everyone who is a parent knows that children completely reshuffle the relationship.

The average age at which a woman in Greece has her first child is over thirty-one, which makes them the oldest first-time mothers in the world. Australia, South Korea, Japan, Italy and Switzerland follow with an average age of thirty. Canada comes in at twenty-third place with an average first birth age of twenty-eight, while the average age in New Zealand, the United Kingdom and Israel stands at twenty-seven. In Ukraine, Sri Lanka and the United States the average goes down to twenty-five, while many African countries have an average age of eighteen for a first pregnancy. The ages of your parents will certainly have an influence on you as the firstborn. One could say: the more life experience, the better. There is no denying that your younger siblings will have had the benefit of 'wiser' parents who knew the ropes thanks to you, their little queen.

## High expectations

Parents who first assume the role of educator are generally found to harbour unrealistically high expectations. They wish to be perfect at their new trade and to turn you into a perfect human specimen. For convenience's sake they temporarily forget that such people do not exist. Everyone is marked by their parents, who weren't perfect either. As the eldest daughter you are the one through whom your parents are discovering a lot not only about raising a child but also about themselves.

Things that, of course, escape your attention as an innocent newborn lying babbling happily in your bouncer. You bask in the undivided attention that is showered upon you. You know precisely how to make Mummy laugh and how to twist your dad around your little finger. You are the one who keeps them on their toes, as you constantly present them with new challenges. They have just grown accustomed to a baby that lies quietly on the bed, when you discover what fun it is to turn over... They need another pair of hands and eyes. They exert themselves finding ways to please you. You are their first, their only child, the sun that all planets revolve around. Nothing needs to change – if it were up to you.

IN BRIEF

- Eldest daughters are the ones who make their parents into parents.
- As the eldest, you enjoy undivided attention for everything you do.
- Your parents wish to get 'it' right and feel insecure because you are a first for them.
- Parents bring their own education with them.
- Parents often have unrealistically high expectations of their firstborn.

# 2

# A solid basis

. . .

**LISETTE** For hours on end, heads close together, my best friend Lineke and I sat poring over the atlas. I dearly wanted to avoid getting another bad mark for my geographic knowledge of my home country, the Netherlands. Why I was so bad at this subject remained a mystery to me because I really paid attention in class, I couldn't sleep if I had not finished my homework and I knew all the names of the major conglomerations of our country by heart. Yet it went wrong time and again. When the teacher pointed his long wooden stick to one city on the big blank map that he had hung at the front of the classroom, I wrote down the name of a town at the other end of the province. I didn't confuse Amsterdam, Rotterdam and the Hague, but pretty much any city smaller in size I just could not identify.

Worried after I had come home crying hot tears about my next bad mark, my mother went to see him. The teacher couldn't help but laugh at how highly protective she was as she stood up for her eldest. Still, he had to concede he was as puzzled as she was: I had a good memory, I did my best, so it was an enigma to both of them that I couldn't seem to master geography. The subject remained a source of stress and sadness for me, until the school doctor came to inspect us on her periodic visit. This formidable woman saved the day: I was nearsighted. I needed glasses.

I was ten, it was 1964 and the choice in spectacle frames was minimal, especially for children. When I got my first set of glasses, the only question was whether I preferred a blue or a red band on the upper part of the frame. I chose the blue as I wanted my glasses to be as inconspicuous as possible. It was bad enough that I needed them in the first place. I was already wearing braces; apparently I had not come into this world flawless, I thought not without shame. I felt sorry for my parents that they had an imperfect daughter who needed so much augmentation. That was surely not how they had imagined me to be.

These corrective devices also emphasized the difference between me and my brother and sister, who needed none at all. They outflanked me socially as, in contrast to me, they made friends easily. Whenever someone in her class had a birthday, my younger sister (by four years) was always invited to go along and celebrate. My brother (two years my junior) horsed about in the schoolyard with boys from the highest grade. They knew everyone at the school and everyone knew them, while I was a shy and serious child with braces, glasses and one best friend.

Later that year the same primary-school teacher picked me for such an honour that I could hardly believe my luck. A Finnish girl who did not speak a word of Dutch had appeared in our class one day. She had moved to the Netherlands with her mother. For love's sake, we giggled among ourselves. Such an adventure was unheard of at that time in the proper little suburb where I grew up – or at least as far as we ten-year-olds knew. Alternating with two other girls, I was asked to teach Maaret our lovely language. Henriëtte and Ingrid ranked as the undisputed top students in our class. They got high marks in every subject, whereas I only scored high in the language department. That I was now grouped with them – I was proud as a peacock.

We took turns sitting at the back of the classroom for an hour to whisper with the Finnish girl while the rest went through the normal routine. The mere assumption that I would easily recoup that hour worked miracles for my self-esteem. I have a clear memory of once jumping around the classroom like a frog to show Maaret the animal that was the main subject of the story we were reading. The teacher raised his eyebrows. Did I have to be so demonstrative? As I recall, I gave him an obnoxious look. How else could I make this clear? Maybe this incident stuck in my memory because for once I broke out of my good girl guise. Being good at languages saved me. Much like the prince who kissed the little frog with the glasses.

## Measuring up

'What do Angela Merkel, Hillary Rodham Clinton, Christine Lagarde, Oprah Winfrey, Sheryl Sandberg, J.K. Rowling and Beyoncé have in common?' was a headline in the English newspaper the *Observer* in 2014. 'Other than riding high in *Forbes*' list of the world's most powerful women,' journalist Tracy McVeigh wrote in answer to her own question, 'they are also all firstborn children in their families. Firstborn children really do excel.'

McVeigh based her article, immediately picked up by media worldwide, on research done by Feifei Bu. Originally from China, she did her PhD at the University of Essex in England on the topic of 'sibling configurations, educational aspiration and attainment'. Using sibling data from the British Household Panel Survey containing 1,503 sibling clusters and 3,552 individuals, she looked at both achievement and aspiration. What she found was that even taking into account parents' education and professional status, firstborn children were seven per cent more likely to aspire to stay on in education than younger siblings. Here's the really interesting thing: firstborn girls were thirteen per cent more ambitious than firstborn boys. These girls are ambitious. They want to get more out of life – and out of themselves. They are more motivated than anyone else, according to Bu, who as it turns out is an eldest daughter too.

In January 2015, economics editor John Haltiwanger summed up a number of scientific findings in this field on Elite Daily, a popular Facebook page with over three million likes. In his piece 'The Science of Superiority: Why the firstborn child is the smartest one', he cites a recent study by the American National Bureau of Economic Research (NBER), which isn't the first one to show that firstborn children do better at school than their younger siblings. One of the most interesting theories argues that the oldest children do better at school because they grow smarter by teaching their young siblings. If you can teach, then you certainly understand and value the power of knowledge, he writes. As another potential factor he cites the 'divorce theory'; simply put, divorce is quite common in today's society, but it's more likely to happen after the first child is born. Thus, the oldest child gets the benefit of not having their upbringing disrupted by a family crisis.

Lucy McCarraher, an expert on work-life balance, adds the practical view of a mother of four, 'All the parents I know agree that the eldest gets more attention because there is more time for them before the next one – or next ones – move up to that stage and need help as well,' this eldest daughter says.

According to V. Joseph Hotz, Arts & Sciences Professor of Economics at Duke University, who was one of the economists to work on the research for the NBER study, however, it all depends on the way in which parents discipline their children. When a child does poorly at school and there are no parental consequences or disciplinary actions, then they won't be motivated to do better. On the basis of empirical studies he advances the theory that firstborns are more likely to face daily homework monitoring than younger siblings. Parents think strategically and the reputation model is at play here; they supervise the eldest child the most in the hopes that younger siblings will observe that lazy school performance leads to closer monitoring or loss of privileges, and will then have additional incentives to do well at school. With the eldest they set the example, is the economists' strategic view.

## Happier than ever

Most parents are over the moon with their first child; her or his arrival has made them happier than they have ever been before in their lives and will ever be again. We're not making this up. The Dutch national statistics agency has conducted research on the correspondence between happiness and having children. In 2013, they published their findings: that people are happiest around the time of having their first child. When asked, thirty-one per cent of the Dutch indicated that they are very happy. In a pregnancy year this percentage goes up drastically; it rises as high as forty-two per cent. Even people who are usually not particularly happy are markedly more joyous in the year in which they or their partner are pregnant for the first time.

The superb mystery, that a new being is created from the merging of two people, in itself brings a sense of bliss to both the man and the woman involved. Yet the effect on the mother-to-be is demonstrably bigger than on the father. The number of women indicating they are very happy in the year before the birth of their first child is forty-five per cent, while it is thirty-nine per cent among men. Apart from the hormones that without a shadow of a doubt are at play, an obvious explanation is that women are constantly aware of the baby because they are the ones who are pregnant. Initially they mostly feel the changes in their own body, which in itself is an incredible experience that first time. Then they progressively begin to notice the baby that is growing so intimately inside them. It turns, it kicks, it gets the hiccups. The father lays a hand on her tummy to get an impression. He feels from the outside, she from the inside. He turns over and goes to sleep, she lies awake with the frolicking. Men can forget temporarily that their whole life is about to change fundamentally. For the woman everything has changed already, from the first moment she found out that she was expecting.

> *'I guess what really forms you as a person is what you do within your family to receive love or attention. In my family, what you had to do to receive attention was to have good conversation at the dinner table or to do well at school, and those were really my focuses because that was what was valued the most.'*
>
> — EMMA WATSON in *GQ*

It used to be – and in some cultures and countries this still is the case – that during a pregnancy hopes are high for the child to be a boy. A father wanted an heir who could carry on the family name, or be a successor to continue the farm, the store or the business. The mother was under pressure to present her husband with a son. There were other practical reasons as well. A boy was an extra hand: a girl meant bending over backwards to supply her with a dowry. In some cultures there is still a high preference for the first child to be a boy. In the United States, if they had the choice most parents would opt for a masculine first child, forty-seven per cent. They assume a boy is easier to raise than a girl. Later, as an older brother, he is a natural protector of their later-borns. A third of Americans indicate that they have no preference when it comes to gender and the remaining twenty-one per cent would most love to have a girl. In the Netherlands, recent new parents who were interviewed by the statistics agency said a daughter or a son would make them equally happy. When asked for a preference most Dutch expectant parents say: 'As long as our child is healthy.'

## Fragile – beware

Each family has its own emotional tone, set by the way the parents relate to one another. The first child often comes into this world at the peak of happiness for the prospective parents. After birth this extraordinary sense of bliss diminishes. The pace at which this happens is equal for both parents but, because the father's sense of happiness had risen less high before the birth, men are the first to arrive back at their old level.

Within a year fathers are as happy as they were before the arrival of their first child. Mothers' extreme sense of bliss generally continues for another two to three years. The exact opposite happens for people who indicate not being overjoyed with being pregnant for the first time: the four per cent saying they are not happy during pregnancy on average become happier once the child is born.

In the meantime, the little one is surrounded with all kinds of care. Bit by bit it picks up all manner of things. Our parents are our role models, after all. They are the first ones we watch to see what it is to be human. In their turn parents attempt to teach their children good behaviour, from smiling when Grandma comes to visit to learning to get your food into your mouth by yourself without splashing it all over you. From your first little words up to being potty trained. You cannot do without this concentrated effort of your parents. Apart from what they try to teach you consciously, the little one picks up all kinds of signals that are never really named. A child not only learns from what the parents do but, even more, from *how* they go about things. Whether they are aware of it or not, as soon as a child is around parents are role models. When they display genuine pleasure and glee upon seeing an aunt come in the door, the child will most likely take this person for someone worthy of their trust and climb on their lap. When they are gentle in their interactions towards one another, the child will also relax. When they take fright, the child that initially remained quiet will burst into tears after all.

In general, parents handle their firstborn with more care than they do the children that follow. By that time they have learned that a child is quite sturdy, that a baby will actually survive when their pureed apple is served a bit later and that they themselves have proved to be capable of parenthood. With their first, however, they tend to be as careful as if the baby could break in two at any minute. The firstborn is not allowed to do all kinds of things out of fear that something untoward might happen. What exactly this untoward thing could be is never quite clarified but in the meantime it hangs like a dark cloud over the child's head. Many eldest children grow into risk-averse adults. They become somewhat more anxious and cautious than others, a tad more careful. The nervousness of the parents about their own capacity to keep such a fragile little being alive is, to a certain extent, absorbed by a first child.

## Smart through attention

Everything to which you give attention grows. In general, the firstborn receives a lot of attention. Every move, every smile, every soiled nappy and each burp in that initial period are regarded as miracles that have surely never occurred before. The first is also given an ocean of time – there is no routine yet for all the kinds of small actions that parents need to perform. Changing a nappy or bottle-feeding their baby can be a hugely time-consuming task. They have to master getting the child in and out of their clothes. To top it off, they want nothing more than to extend the close special time they are able to spend with their newborn. Every moment is precious. A baby is so special and grows so terribly fast and the new parents want to witness your every smile, each small step in your development. This time is all for the firstborn. They are such a miracle, such a source of love and delight. Whatever stress the day brings, as soon as the baby enters the picture, parents remember what their efforts are all for. For him or her.

From the start, the child relishes this undivided attention, which also helps in its growth. It is, after all, through observing and imitation that we as humans develop. This begins as soon as the little one is born. Neural networks are being laid down at a furious pace in the fast-growing brain to process and retain information. Each day brings new opportunities for further growth. During the first weeks, months and sometimes even years, the first child is mainly surrounded by adults and it absorbs more information from them than they may take into account.

> '*I am incredibly proud of my daughters. Tiger parenting is about assuming strength rather than weakness in our children and basically helping them be the best they can be. Teaching them that they are capable of so much more and not allowing them to give up.*'
>
> — AMY CHUA on *Today.com*

This results in the eldest developing an above-average intelligence, as was shown in a Norwegian study, published in 2007 in the renowned magazine *Science*. The average IQ worldwide is between 90 and 110; this study found that firstborns come out with a two to three points higher score. Three points on an IQ test may not sound like much, but experts say it can be a tipping point for some people. Renowned UC Berkeley researcher Dr Frank J. Sulloway, who wrote a commentary accompanying the study, noted that two to three IQ points could translate to an added twenty to thirty points on an SAT college entrance exam. 'You go to a certain school, meet a famous professor, and the next thing you know, you've gone on to medical school, made a great discovery and won the Nobel Prize,' said Sulloway, who is the author of *Born to Rebel: Birth Order, Family Dynamics and Creative Lives.* He goes on to calculate that a 2.3 IQ score difference means that the eldest child has a thirteen per cent higher chance of having above-average intelligence than the second-born in their family.

This settles an age-old debate on why the majority of illustrious prizes such as the Swedish Nobel Prize are awarded to authors and scientists who are the eldest children in their family. Just as there are more eldest children who, on the grounds of their achievements, win scholarships in the United States. Surely it cannot be due to a whim of nature that intelligence is distributed among birth positions in unequal measure?

Now we may, of course, be biased and we haven't deeply researched the intelligence levels of middle and youngest children, which we don't at all want to discount. We mean to shed light on patterns in the lives of the eldest, not to polarize. Dr Petter Kristensen, who led the Norwegian study, is a second child himself. He did not attach an ounce of credibility to the theory of the effects of birth order. This was not the focus of his research either; he just wanted to find out how reliable IQ tests actually were. His data came from the Norwegian army, which has been putting all their new recruits through an IQ test for years. Kristensen and his team compared the results of 240,000 boys of eighteen and nineteen years of age over a period of twenty years. The analysis produced an undeniable result. The eldest son scored higher than the second-born, who in turn scored higher than the third-born. Thus Kristensen hit on the influence of birth order in spite of himself. He, too, attributes the difference partially to the fact that the eldest receives more focused attention.

It is discouraging at times to see how many studies are done on boys and men. For his hefty book, Sulloway, who gave such a pointed comment on the Norwegian study, combed through thousands of biographies of people influential in politics, science and religion. He took a deep dive into history and thus into the lives of men – who until recently were the ones running the show. Can eldest daughters also stake a claim to having a higher than average intelligence because this has been found to be the case for eldest sons?

Maybe that is the reason that Feifei Bu's findings were picked up so widely by media across the globe. From the *Daily Mail* and the *Japan Times* to the *New Zealand Herald*, and of course on the Internet. After all the studies that for years have been done exclusively on boys and men, she at last showed how motivated and capable eldest daughters are.

## Eloquent and articulate

Bu attributes the higher ambition and eagerness to learn of eldest daughters to that first period of undivided parental attention. Many deem this also to be the basis of another phenomenon: although not markedly better than later-born children in maths and other subjects, eldest children excel noticeably in languages. There is no real explanation other than the fact that as an infant the eldest is mostly surrounded by adults. The toddler saves all that it hears in its young brain, even if it doesn't have a clue what the conversations are about. Then when it first mumbles something that sounds a bit like 'Mummy', the parents rejoice.

For a child this is not a personal tribute to her first and foremost caretaker. After the initial 'ah', 'eh', 'oh' and 'uh' sounds that babies on all continents produce, a baby that follows a normal pattern of development will begin to crow with pleasure. Then from the age of around seven months, baby-talk can be heard from the crib. According to researchers the m-sound is easy to make for the unpractised mouth and so 'mummmm' is among the first words a little one produces. It is an involuntary evolutionary step. The baby has no clue what it means but nature has arranged it so that as a mother you are maximally motivated at such a moment to take care of your child. By hearing you seemingly speaking her name, she feels even more attached to you than ever.

Soon you're able to say more. Time and time again you are requested to repeat your first little words, and each time your parents respond with equal glee and pride. Your granny and your grandpa, uncles and aunts, friends of your parents, the neighbours: they must all come and hear this. Whether you are early or late to start to talk, you're being proudly displayed: 'Listen to what our little one is already able to do!' You melt the grown-ups' hearts and they want to hear your full repertoire once more. They clap their hands when you seem to call them by their names. 'What a clever little thing you are!' All this makes talking into something for you to feel proud of. Each time you have learned to say something new, there is someone around to praise and hug you. Talking, in your book, starts to equal receiving positive attention and this is the best encouragement to continue down this road.

> *'I love to win Oscars. Love it. The only part about it I don't like is the red carpet and getting a dress and walking around in high heels and holding in my stomach. I hate that.'*
> — SHIRLEY MACLAINE on *imdb.com*

In her book *Lean in: Women, Work, and the Will to Lead* Facebook's COO Sheryl Sandberg, the eldest of three, also addresses this point. She quotes recent research done in the United States that shows that parents tend to talk more with their daughters than with their sons. Boys are generally allowed to go off on their own to play at an earlier age than girls. The sons also tend to be given instructions on how to behave, while the daughters are engaged in conversation. It also appears that mothers conduct more emotionally complex conversations with their daughters, which causes them to develop the vocabulary of feeling.

Thus a natural self-perpetuating effect is brought into being. Mastering languages may become part of your self-image. You pick up the language of the adults around you, you are showered with attention when you astound them with your vocabulary, you think you are extraordinarily gifted in the languages department and therefore you become it. This may be another reason why girls tend to perform better than boys at school and in their later studies.

## Outperforming statistics

Parents usually have high expectations of their firstborn child. Unrealistically high expectations. They are astounded by the miracle that you are and assume that the apple of their eye will astound others just as much. Even if they will never admit it, they tend to think that their baby will outperform all measurements and statistics.

It goes without saying that objectively you are just more beautiful; that their first one will also be potty trained earlier than an average child; and that you will be able to walk and to talk sooner than others. This sounds like a joke but it holds a kernel of truth. It is precisely because parents experience it all for the first time that they require assurance that they are getting things right. Statistics may satisfy them to a point, but the real assurance has to come from their own child, who has to be the living proof that he or she is as exceptional and gifted as the parents think.

A child craves the approval of its parents. It doesn't want to put the love and care it receives at risk. Even at this very young age there is an instinctive awareness that parents are necessary for all manner of things. The little one will not make it on its own and so it wants nothing more than to rise to expectations, however sky-high and unrealistic these might be. A child is in no position to gauge this at this point, and so it makes an attempt. Or it doesn't.

Some eldest daughters cave in under the pressure they feel from their parents. If they feel they cannot live up to the high standards that are being set, they would rather give up before getting started. This unwitting choice may lead to a life full of more or less deliberate failures and missed opportunities. During our research, several second-born daughters told us stories of how their older sister somehow always ended up sabotaging her own life. Her stubborn refusal to step into her own is like that of a well-trained horse that stops right in front of an obstacle and cannot be cajoled into jumping. More often than not the second daughter then assumes the role of the serious achiever.

In spite of changing ideas on being the heir, eldest sons of course have to deal with high expectations as well. Some live up to it, many find their own way and others try to avoid the load they feel is put on them. When they step away, the younger sister may still develop into a kind of eldest daughter. Her starting position differs from a real eldest, not merely because the peak in parents' happiness seems to be reserved for the time around the birth of the first child. No such peak has been found to occur around the birth of the second or the third child. When parents are extra happy before the arrival of number two, this seems to be the afterglow of the birth of the first child. This one, however, is in for a life-changing event: she will have to share her undisputed place in the sun. What impact does this have on her?

## IN BRIEF

- Parents are happiest around the birth of their first child.
- Parents tend to expect that their little miracle will outperform statistics.
- Parents are more careful in their handling of a firstborn than they are with later children.
- The undivided attention is what makes eldest children more intelligent.
- Generally speaking, eldest children will be better at verbal communication than the others.
- Eldest children tend to be more eager to learn than other children and perform better at school.
- By being harsh with their eldest child, parents hope to set an example for the rest.

3.

# Number two – what to do?

• • •

What to do when you are two and you get a sister? I don't re-member. I see photos of myself in which I am deftly helping my mother bathe a little girl. Just like other parents, mine must have thought it would be good to engage me as much as possible in caring for the new baby. I cannot remember specific instances, but I do recall a certain feeling. This feeling might best be described as anxiety, even though I find it strange to speak about anxiety in a toddler. Yet I am sure I am not making this up. I see it in the photos: in my somewhat protective or patronizing attitude towards her. In one of those old pictures I hold her close while we both wobble in a pair of wooden clogs. Her hand grabs my dress tightly.

There is also a photo of both of us in my kindergarten classroom where she was allowed in briefly to see her own future classroom. I bend over her, one hand on her belly, the other presumably at her back. She looks around with an air of wonder. Also when she had really grown out of it, I put her into a pram. In the photo I hold its handlebar, while she sits there laughing and pretending to read a comic book. We are both smiling a lot in these old pictures but she is always the one making funny faces. She acted the fool, while I was quite seriously concerned with what we were going to play next.

One photo has us both in ballet costumes: she looks very lovely, I am somewhat straight and shapeless. This one was taken before a per-formance at primary school in which we danced to the music of Abba. I gave myself fully to the dance – and later found out my costume had not been zipped up at the back. My sister took ballet lessons, she was better at it than me and yet she deferred to me. I have never given this a thought until now, really. It was a given to me that she would listen to me sweetly.

This is almost painful to concede now that I can see how fully I behaved in line with the patterns we found in the various studies on the effects of birth order. I was the eldest and the wisest, she the youngest and the witty one. That is also the way people would view us. I remember an instance when we went hiking in the mountains with my father and my aunt. My sister took a liking to a tree trunk three times the size of her small body and merrily dragged it along. When my father wanted to take her picture, she made a silly face that had us all in stitches. We tried to convince her to leave the huge thing behind, but she wouldn't hear of it. Then, suddenly, she caught up with us, having let go in her own good time. While I all the time had been keeping pace with my father like a serious and wise adult.

The day came when my sister no longer enjoyed my interfering eldest-sister ways. It took me a while to comprehend. I did not understand it right away because I was not at all aware of the pattern – it had been so familiar to me for such a long time. Now we are both adult women with busy lives and families of our own. The roles we play in life have changed, but one glance at a childhood photo and the old feeling of anxiety springs to life.

## Off the throne

The skies are blue. There is not a cloud in sight. You have a father and a mother who dote on you. They delight in your every new discovery and applaud each accomplishment. You are their little queen, and you love sitting on your velvet throne. Then one day, clouds start to gather on the horizon. Your parents become just a bit less attentive in catering to your every need. Your mother keeps rubbing her tummy and suddenly she cannot wrap you up in her arms as easily as she used to. Your father keeps alluding to the wonderful new sister or brother who is soon to arrive on the scene. 'Just a few more weeks now, sweetie.'

You feel that something is about to change, even if you may not be able to fathom exactly what it is. You trust all will be well. Until you discover that out of the clouds in the sky, lightning has struck, in the form of a small creature. What is happening here? This wonderful new sibling your father alluded to proves to be outrageously demanding. Why is he or she allowed to be with Mummy all the time? Was that not your place? What is this intruder doing in your life? Lightning has hit indeed.

There are no two ways about it. With the arrival of a sibling, all of a sudden you are the eldest and this means you have to come off the throne you occupied unequivocally as the princess you were as an only child. That is a shame because you really liked it high up there. Until now you had your parents at your beck and call. All your firsts were a first for them, too. However insecure and inexperienced they may have felt, they could not believe their good fortune when you saw the light of day. You had not just your room, your bed and your toys all to yourself, you had these grown-ups to yourself as well. You were the undisputed queen in the household. Who would want to give that up? Not you – but you will have to. From now on you will have to share with this newcomer who seems so helpless, this baby who gets an inordinate amount of attention. Not just from your parents but also from visitors, who bend over the crib cooing and wooing. OK, they bring a present for you but you're no fool. An occasional gift in no way makes up for the sense of dethronement that you are experiencing. It is no wonder that, as little as you are, you have a deep reaction to this crucial change in your life.

Edith Neisser in her 1957 book *The eldest child* gives a wonderfully witty description of the feelings the first child must experience when confronted with the arrival of another baby. 'The feelings of the first-born have often been compared to the feelings a wife would have if her husband told her: "I love you so much, I think it would be twice as nice to have two wives". Both situations entail the indignity and discomfort of having only a half interest in the person who is vital to your well-being.'

Add to that the fact that affection, to a child, feels like a cake – every time someone else gets a piece, she imagines that much less remains for her – and all the ingredients for the drama are present. You do not like this little interloper. You think there will not be enough time left for you. All the affection given to the baby is taken from the attention your mummy and your daddy are able to show to you. It does not make a difference that this doom scenario will not play out fully as most parents do realize they should pay some extra attention to their eldest when number two has arrived.

The child's experience is painful. You feel bereft and you are not going to count the hours they spend on the other child. If you had, you would be in for a surprise. In *The F1rstborn Advantage* Kevin Leman cites a study from Brigham Young University in which the researchers kept a record that showed that between the ages of four and thirteen, the firstborn is given more quality time by their parents than later-borns receive at the same age. This is not an hour or two: it is in fact three thousand hours more.

## Green with envy

Envy is a feeling familiar to all of us. We are taught not to have it, or at least not to show it, but it is still there, and suppressing it or denying it is usually useless. For an eldest, envy is bound to be part of life. How else could you respond to the sudden turnaround in your fortunes? What is wrong with you, you'll wonder? Why did they have to have another? You were having a good time together with the three of you, weren't you? Psychologists point out that initial signals of envy can be observed when the arrival of a brother or sister is imminent. Many of us were about two at the time when lightening hit. With envy come feelings, reactions and thoughts. What those are depends largely on factors such as your temperament, the amount of self-esteem you have built up and how much understanding you have of what is happening around you during the new pregnancy and after the sibling is born.

The nasty feeling can only arise when there is someone to be envious of. Not every child will react in the same way and age plays an important part. As a two-year-old girl you have just started to walk and talk and begun to gain independence; you exercise your will by saying no so often that it can drive your parents to distraction.

Just imagine the overstretched parent who does not have enough eyes and hands to keep the situation under control. My goodness, you were sitting a moment ago, now you run off towards the sea – and oh, what are you doing waving that knife about? Or the way child psychologists and educators see it: two is the age at which a child starts to risk conflicts with its parents to gain a measure of independence. The arrival of another child doesn't help. The time in which you could be alone with your parents and receive their full attention has suddenly been drastically diminished – and on top of that, they are also telling you not to touch things. Could it be that your parents like you less now that you move about so independently and resolutely?

Lisette noticed some years ago that she tended to be somewhat subdued when the whole family was gathered together. On the rare occasions that she had her father, now deceased, and mother to herself, she found she couldn't stop talking about her life. 'It was an interesting moment when I realized how free and happy I felt when it was just the three of us, the original triangle of our family. I felt completely at ease much like – I imagine – I did before my two brothers and my sister came to break open our "holy trinity" and change my life for ever.'

> 'My brother was an amazing cat. He was the funny one in the family.'
>
> —— WHOOPI GOLDBERG on *The View*

Illustrator and author Jan Ormerod grew up in Australia as the youngest of four sisters. A mother of two daughters herself, she brought a fresh vision to children's picture books with her luminous images, storytelling genius and understanding of how children behave. Her sweet book *The Baby Swap* shows the anguish of the eldest daughter. 'This baby brother is not at all what I want,' Caroline Crocodile said. 'He is smelly and dribbly, he is no fun and takes up all the room on my mother's lap. I would like to swap him for one that is exactly right.'

Research indicates that when a second child is born eldest girls often respond with a kind of sadness, while boys will be more inclined to thrash about, get into fights and break their toys. The boys throw their unhappiness outside, while girls generally act more cautiously. They are apt to swallow their confusing and often conflicting emotions and pretend all is well. To show feelings of anger openly feels dangerous somehow now that the whole family situation has changed so drastically overnight. Being sensitive to the fact that her parents find their new child adorable, the young girl will look for other ways to approach the issue. A three-year-old who had had her fill of the little howler put her small sister into the wastepaper basket. Now life could revolve around her again. Another eldest daughter admitted only recently to something many of us must have done: pinching the little one hard when she thought no one was looking. The baby, of course, immediately started to howl and the mother was somewhat suspicious: 'Did you touch her?' What do you do as the eldest? You look your mother in the eye and plead your innocence.

## Proud girl

The parents' attitude is paramount. Parents want to guide their first child through this time of turbulence as best they can. They may be disappointed when they see that their firstborn is not overjoyed with the new, delightful baby. This shatters the idyllic image of the perfect happy family. Their eldest, their unquestioned prodigy, changes into an unmanageable hothead before their very eyes. Sometimes the eldest reverts to behaviour it had grown out of. This is the phenomenon of regression. The apple of their eye, who is already potty trained, suddenly is so no more, to the despair of the parents who had welcomed this new phase. Or, suddenly, she has decided she wants to be given the bottle again, safely on her mother's lap.

Age is very important too. The younger you were when your brother or sister was born, the more concrete and simple were your conclusions: less attention for you just meant they liked you less. So the longer you had had as an only child, being read to, or to put it another way the bigger the slice of the aforementioned cake was given to you, the more loved you felt.

It is not easy for parents to explain to a two-year-old that they really have to feed the baby first before they can get her a rice-cake. Yet, as a parent you want nothing more than to be there for your jealous elder one. Even when she is not being very demonstrative about it – or when she is a bit older and understands more – you try to divide your attention as best you can. Unfortunately, jealous children are impeccable in their timing. They keep quiet when the baby is asleep in their crib, but the minute you need your full motherly focus on the newborn your eldest makes the nefarious plan to smear the wall with jam. As a mother, what are you to do? Exactly – you tell her off. Giving her the loving attention that an eldest craves at moments like this is just not always in your gift.

A method many parents revert to is to engage their eldest in caring for the young one. This way she can be shown that she still fully belongs. Often this goes hand in hand with praising her for what she can do in comparison to the helpless little creature she is not showing much fondness for yet. Many photos of eldest daughters are of a proud girl with a serious expression on her face, bottle-feeding the tiny one or putting her hand in the bath to feel if the temperature is right. Less responsible actions such as allowing your eldest to throw too many sweets into the shopping trolley, of course, also occur.

It may help young parents to realize that with small children a harmonious and quiet life sometimes just is not within the realm of possibility. The crying is loud, food is being thrown in all directions and sometimes you are exhausted from lack of sleep. At these times, you might yourself be just a tad jealous of your childless friend who departs for a four-week holiday. Just like your own eldest daughter who is learning that life can be wonderful one moment and somewhat less joyous the next. Allow her to have her reaction. Openly jealous behaviour, unless it is taken to an extreme, is quite normal in this phase. In most cases it disappears of its own accord after a while. Most important of all is to let her, your eldest, feel how much you love her. Due to the hectic pace of daily life you're bound to forget to do this sometimes, but a child never tires of hearing you say you love her.

*'Watching Chelsea mother Charlotte is just the greatest joy and I could not be more impressed by or excited for Charlotte and the new baby because they have the best mother in the world.'*
— HILLARY RODHAM CLINTON on *YouTube*

## You're a big girl now

What happens to you, as the eldest daughter, when your parents allow you to help them in all that needs doing to keep the busy household running? When you are allowed to do more and more by yourself because you are a big girl already? Apart from fathers and mothers engaging your help to make you feel that you fully belong, they will also have done so out of necessity. Conjure up the image of a mother with a baby in one arm while clutching the phone under her chin and desperately trying to button up the coat of her eldest. She notices she might be doing something that is no longer necessary. Next time she decides to do what parents have done through the ages: she lets her eldest button up her own coat and praises her to the heavens.

This is the predicament of the modern multitasking mother trying to keep her own work on track and raise her children at the same time. You could compare her to the mother in former times, who often would not work in the outside world but who had to run a laborious household mostly on her own while her husband went out to earn the money. These mothers, too, were forced to call on their firstborn.

Examples from eldest daughters who were given responsibilities at a young age prove not hard to find. An eldest daughter from a family of nine told us how one day her mother transferred all the care of sister number five to her. From that day onwards it was more or less taken for granted that she took care of this sister. Only much later in their adult lives were these two able to reflect together on their relationship as sisters and from then on they agreed to do things differently.

Even in smaller families parents regularly call on the eldest to hold the baby for a minute or to stand obediently with the buggy while they run back to the house to grab a dummy. Or to pay attention in the public pool when the youngest is still unable to swim. For a busy mum these might look like little tasks, but many eldest daughters vividly remember these occurrences later in life as huge responsibilities. Even when as a parent you have resolved not to burden your daughter by making her responsible too often, life has a way of sneaking it in anyway.

A somewhat different outlook on the responsibilities of children is given by writer Tom Hodgkinson. He holds the opinion that we worry way too much about the happiness of our children these days. In 2009, he wrote the witty book *The Idle Parent*, which is a plea for lazy parenthood. He recalls how he himself discovered one day that as a freelancer he had his best ideas while lying in bed in the morning. Of course, this would be judged by the outside world as being 'lazy'.

This realization prompted him to enquire into what is thought of as lazy from another angle. As a father of three children under ten years of age, he describes himself as an overanxious parent who wants to stimulate his children in every which way and give them his full attention. What would happen, he wondered, if he let his children be for a while, allowing them to take matters into their own hands; if he should change into an idle parent? What he found was that the child learns to look after itself; it grows in self-esteem and becomes more self-reliant. His advice therefore is: leave your children alone. Give them a chance to discover the ways of the world for themselves. Let them help with the washing-up, cooking and gardening.

Realize that until at least the age of four, children see everything as a game, including tasks that many adults don't much enjoy. Interestingly enough this has also been what many eldest daughters have had to do, of course: wash up, hold the little one and mow the lawn. Whether we have always seen this as a game, even when we were less than four years old, would be a good subject for a chat with Mr Hodgkinson, but he does have a point with this concept of learning to trust your child and leaving it to its own devices. Most parents only allow their firstborn more freedom out of necessity caused by the birth of the next one. For then there is no other way.

## Leader or pleaser?

Eldest daughters are often categorized as one of two: the leader, or the carer or pleaser. The leader is the one who loves to be in charge. The carer or pleaser is always engaged in making others happy.

Experience tells us that eldest daughters may also, to a certain degree, fill both roles at the same time. You can be a leader who feels responsible for the suffering in the world and displays a huge level of care. Lisette is a good example. When it comes to small acts, she would not describe herself as a carer; she tends to forget that a neighbour is ill or a friend might need or like a phone call to cheer them. Yet to her own surprise, when it comes to the bigger picture, she is often asked out of the blue to be the leader or the chairperson of an initiative. She wholeheartedly cares for those in the organizations she leads.

Wies, on the other hand, does not consider herself to be a leader. She loves to cook, to care for those around her. She has had to learn the hard way that you can only truly care for others if you take care of yourself. In the kitchen however, she is in command like the captain of a ship. When she is present and something needs doing, she will volunteer. Without being aware of it, she behaves like any other leader. In brief, one can say that psychologists sketch the extremes: you are either a leader or a carer. That is useful to the extent that you will probably recognize a bit more of yourself in one type than the other, but in practice there are a zillion interesting variations.

The leader who grows out of a firstborn is not by definition a natural talent. Some are, of course, but chances are that circumstances have forced you to become more resolute. You had, after all, become used to being the centre of attention in that first period alone with your parents. All eyes were on you even when you did no more than move your pinkie finger. To retain that attention it seemed a good idea to steal the show whenever possible. Does trying to climb a chair bring smiles to the faces of the grown-ups? Well, then you will do it again and again. Maybe folding your chubby arms the way your mother does with hers will make them admire you as well. Your aim as a little one is to do what it takes to remain in control. When you are always the first to attempt something new, you are again the focus of all attention; it is a simple ploy.

Maybe not right after your brother or sister was born, but soon afterwards you will probably be the one who makes up a charade at Christmas or takes the lead in bringing your mother breakfast in bed on her birthday on a wobbly tray. Long into adulthood younger siblings with a laugh – or spite – enjoy telling the story of what you as a little leader had them do. Similarly, when at school a question is being asked, you will often want to be the first one to answer or come up with the solution.

Your bossy behaviour may have you squashing others while you remain oblivious of the fact that you are pre-empting your younger sibling's or classmate's turn. They, too, would like to show off what they can do and who they are. Yet as an eldest daughter you are often completely in the dark about your bossiness. You think it is only right to take the lead; it makes you feel that you are someone, that you matter. You are therefore disappointed when people don't value everything that you make happen. You are completely immersed in doing things well and unaware that others may find you overpowering.

> *'I am focused on the work. I am constantly creating. I am a busy girl. I live and breathe my work. I love what I do. I believe in the message. There's no stopping.'*
>
> — LADY GAGA on *Goodreads.com*

If you are a carer or a pleaser, then as an eldest daughter you must unconsciously have drawn the conclusion that you would win your parents over by being good to others. You love nothing better than to fuss around and you aim for peace and harmony. You are the eldest daughter who at age eight would stand in the kitchen to make dinner for your mother, who was ill, and the rest of the family. The one who does her utmost to get high marks at school, as you are fully aware that this pleases your father no end. You try to do well for everybody and only later will you find out that you have set yourself an impossible task. First, of course, it is the approval of your father and mother that you crave; later you seek this approval from people around you with a certain degree of authority. For instance, as soon as you notice that a teacher likes you, sees who you are and what you are able to do, you thrive and adore them.

Eldest daughters with a critical father and/or mother run the risk of becoming insecure about their place in the world. This may also come to pass when your parents, out of love, have wanted to protect you from all the mistakes they themselves have made, and have thus continually criticized you – in loving or not so loving ways – for your misdeeds. This has made you grow into someone who does not think very highly of herself. A person who may be incredibly successful in the eyes of others but inwardly always feels she doesn't really amount to much. As a pleaser you will also want to avoid being the one who disturbs the harmony and this tendency has you doing things that in your heart of hearts you don't really want to do. In that case you are easy prey for those who want to make use of you. For pleasers it is of paramount importance to realize that the first one you need to please is you.

## Grandmothers and others

What can be marvellous for eldest daughters is for another member of the family to look out for her while her parents have their hands full with number two. Grandmother, grandfather, an aunt, an uncle or even a teacher or the neighbours can fit the bill. Eldest daughters, when asked about a favourite person in their lives, mention a host of kind and patient grannies, sweet aunts and exceptional teachers with whom they formed a special bond that they often maintain in their adult lives. Wies remembers how her aunt always made herself available to her, how this aunt noticed what she did and that in her grown-up years she still hears the voice of this aunt, now deceased, speaking words of encouragement to her. A fond memory that Lisette as an active aunt aspires to live up to.

Another aspect that the eldest has to deal with is that thanks to the arrival of another baby, there is now material for comparisons to be made. Parents have a strong tendency to compare their children. The blonde curls of your sister seem to be a well-loved subject of admiration when people come to admire the new baby. This does not go unnoticed by the eldest child. Do they think she is more beautiful, the eldest wonders? What is wrong with my dark hair? When you are old enough to understand what is being said and a tactless aunt exclaims that your sister really is a beauty, with a compassionate glance at your dark ponytail that you are so proud of, it can stay with you for years and years. As an eldest daughter hopefully you had parents who responded to such situations with patience and with love. To compensate, they probably spoke highly of all your wonderful accomplishments. These words of praise have in turn stimulated you to try even harder than you were already. For this was one of your solutions to the new-baby conundrum: to try your utmost so that your parents would be happy and not forget you were there.

## IN BRIEF

- Dethronement is what it is aptly called: the moment number two arrives and the only child becomes the eldest.
- Girls often swallow their inevitable feelings of jealousy, while boys tend to react by breaking things.
- As an eldest daughter, in all kinds of ways, consciously and unconsciously, your parents will give you responsibilities.
- Between the ages of four and thirteen, firstborns spend more quality time with their parents than their younger siblings do at the same age: 3,000 hours more.
- Eldest daughters often turn out to be leaders and carers at the same time.
- 'Me? Bossy?' Eldest daughters can be quite bossy without being the least bit aware of it.
- Many an eldest daughter will perennially think that whatever she does will never be enough.

# 4.

# Diametrically different

. . .

**LISETTE** I could not believe my eyes when I first met my brother's girlfriend, the woman he would marry. She looked exactly like me. We were equally tall and thin. We wore our hair the same way. More than that, however, I recognized something utterly familiar in her eyes. We were cast in the same mould. How was that possible?

There is no one in the world about whom I have thought and pondered as much as the brother who came into this world two years after me. How could it be that he was so different from me, so unpredictable, disobedient and obstinate at times. Maybe as a child you also imagined a good fairy offering you the fulfilment of three wishes. I could spend hours on end at this game. The first two wishes were crystal clear to me. I would like to be dead for a while so I would know what was in store on the other side of life. I had a hard time deciding how long this temporary death should be. A day seemed too short, two a bit scary. Would I be able to return? Getting the shivers was, of course, part of the attraction of this fantasy. I made the same deliberations for my second wish: that I could be my brother so I could find out from the inside what made him tick. His contrary temperament made no sense to me. I remained puzzled and mesmerized by him then, and also later when we both attended high school and subsequently went on to university, when he went to study abroad. Then he came home with the fair Norwegian Anne-Marie, who within a split second had become as close to me as my real sister and with whom I developed such a deep friendship that she asked me to be her maid of honour at their wedding.

They had four children together. Then she, who had become a bosom friend of both my sister and me, fell ill. She died in 2001. A new woman appeared in the lives of my brother and his young children, who had all of course been heartbroken by their mother's early death. Just like Anne-Marie, Martine is an eldest daughter. She pulled the whole family through. She attended the Eldest Daughter Day. In the words of my brother: 'I have been fortunate with the women in my life.' This I can only agree with, thinking of his wife and partner– and then I add my mother, myself, my sister and his daughters.

## A child already

One in five children remain alone, an only child. The other four eventually obtain a different status: they become the eldest. The second child is born into a different family than the first. The parents might be the same people but they have in the time before the second is born undergone quite a shift. They have turned into parents. This they've learned from you, their firstborn. You were their guinea pig, their sampler. Nowadays many people are mindful of the gap between their first and second children – and nature has a hand in this, too, of course. In the United States the average age gap between siblings is about two and a half years; in Britain, according to research, this average has risen by five months since 2009, with parents now leaving an average of three years and eight months between their children. In these intense years parents have adjusted the towering expectations they held of their prodigy. They have also become more realistic about themselves, they have got to know one another better when it comes to parenting and they have more or less adjusted their lifestyle to having children. Additionally, they have become a bit older and potentially wiser.

Number two arrives into that setting. In his renowned book *Brothers and Sisters: The Order of Birth in the Family*, published at the end of the fifties, anthroposophist Karl König expresses a sense of compassion for the second child who, upon their arrival on earth, finds another child already present within the family. This second one will never truly have time alone with the parents; even if you as the eldest daughter are off to daycare or maybe school during the week while the little one is still at home, your presence will be perceptible all the time. You have to be taken to and collected from wherever you are, so it is your schedule that dictates the order of the day; things have to be bought or arranged for you – but it isn't only because of practicalities that the second is never completely alone with the parents. The eldest child is inseparably ingrained on the hearts and minds of them both. As the eldest daughter you are always there, even when you're not.

## Intuitive psychologists

However happy parents are with their second child, they will never welcome it with as much enchantment as they did you, their eldest daughter. A new baby, while different and special in its own way, is not quite so brand-new the second time round. This is the harsh truth. For you, too, as the firstborn this may be a harsh time. A mother of two daughters only realized after a while that the story she was telling people about the easy birth of the second one might be impacting her eldest unfavourably. Former primary teacher turned parenting expert, author Michael Grose says: 'Children are good observers but lousy interpreters.' So a toddler hearing her mother delight in the easy de-livery of her second child may well conclude that her own birth was difficult. Although there is no need whatsoever for a child to feel guilty or rueful about this, a little one might do just that.

Modern research shows that babies are influenced emotionally from a very young age; from their seventh or eighth month children are visibly attuned to the emotions of the adults around them. At nine months they start to cooper-ate actively when being fed, bathed and dressed. They wave when someone makes ready to leave and, long before they can speak, they understand the in-tention behind words and behaviour. In their second year of life they start to understand what makes parents happy or sad. They may not be able to speak, but there is no doubt that they are aware of when someone close to them is unhappy. This shows when, as small as they are, they make attempts to dispel the sadness. When there is a fight in the house, they themselves become more aggressive; when harmony rules they are happy and sweet. Day to day they learn at their parents' knee what is customary in their family. So it is no wonder that they are also keenly aware if the attention that once naturally all came their way is suddenly diverted.

The French professor in child psychology, Marcel Rufo, rages against the modern habit of engaging children too much in their parents' lives. One of the worst things you can do, according to him, is to take your child with you when you go for an ultrasound. He calls it almost incestuous to have your little one take a peek into the mother's womb. Pointing the growing foetus out on the picture you bring home is enough, he states, and then shower the child with love to reassure it that there is room enough for two in your heart – even when you have doubts about this yourself. How can you ever love your second child as much as you love your first?

> *'My father passed away after a debilitating disease. As the eldest, I had to support my mother and my brothers. So there was empowerment that resulted from his passing, and terrible sorrow and grief, which never goes away.'*
>
> — CHRISTINE LAGARDE in *The Washington Post*

Susan Carey, a professor of psychology at Harvard University studying conceptual change in children between four and twelve years old, calls this age the phase of intuitive psychology. In her book *Conceptual Change in Childhood* (1985), she shows that the explanatory system in which wants and beliefs account for actions is well established by the age of four. 'Infants are endowed with the tools to build an intuitive psychology, just as they are endowed with the tools to build intuitive mechanics and a human language.'

At a young age children also start to make comparisons between how they and others are treated. 'Why is he allowed to do that?' she will enquire when her parents give her younger brother permission to do something that she learned was forbidden, or at least unwished-for. 'Why do I have to go to sleep and he doesn't?' she'll wail later that same day. She will compare herself continually with the infant. For her peace of mind it is desirable that this comparison comes out to her advantage.

The Austrian psychiatrist Alfred Adler was one of the first, a century ago, to recognize the way in which birth order affects personality – an indelible stamp, he called it. He also coined the term 'inferiority complex' as he was the first to notice that we all at times tend to feel less valued than others. For one person this might not hold true as much as for the next one and there certainly are times in our lives when we thrive, but all of us without exception occasionally compare ourselves with others and don't always come out on top. We compensate for this sense of inferiority by pretending to be better. Thus we continually switch from one extreme to the other. To apply this to the eldest: when she feels she is liked less now the new baby is born, then she will take pains to show off her prowess and attract the attention of her parents. Beneath her histrionics lies her desire to remind herself that she is definitely superior to that dribbling intruder.

Sometimes an eldest in her struggle to safeguard her place will move in the opposite direction: despite having been potty trained, all of a sudden she wets her bed again and even wets herself. She demands fiercely to sit on Mummy's lap and be fed from a bottle. Out of sheer jealousy she wants to become as small again as the newborn. Although their previously wonderful eldest daughter severely tries parental patience, her envy is quite natural, of course. It would be more worrying if she were to pretend that nothing was the matter with her.

Rufo recommends that parents allow their daughter to convey to them what is bothering her, while realizing that this very envy helps her to start to distinguish between who she is and who she is not. The rivalry, however difficult we find this emotion, is the cement of the self-image we all must construct at some point. It shows you where you are different and what is yours to do, so you grow into who you essentially are. In this way number one pushes off against number two while number two endeavours to catch up with number one. At the same time, and often to the utter amazement of the parents, they are two utterly different individuals.

## 85 per cent different

Anyone who has been working from the assumption that children from the same family are more or less the same had better think again. The premise that siblings feel alike, share interests or respond similarly to the experiences their parents offer them is a misconception. Children of the same parents may resemble one another physically, but most brothers and sisters are very different when it comes to personality, talent, emotional security, confidence and style.

To begin with the nature component: siblings are family in the first degree. This means that on average they share fifty per cent of their genes. This often is visible in factors such as physique and height, the colour of the eyes and whether or not they turn grey at an early age. One half of their DNA is the same, but the other half being different is enough in itself to generate huge differences. This is wittily described by Amy Chua, the John M. Duff Professor of Law at Yale Law School who is best known for her 2011 book *Battle Hymn of the Tiger Mother*, which both shocked and fascinated parents worldwide.

In her attempt to answer the question of why Chinese parents raise such stereotypically successful children, she ignited a global debate on parenting. The eldest of four sisters herself, Chua was raised to excel and she tells the story of how she in turn brought up her daughters Sophia and Lulu. There is a marked difference, though, between her two daughters. Sophia, her first, displays a rational temperament and exceptional powers of concentration from birth onwards. She sleeps through the night and cries only when it serves a purpose. Later she shows herself to be intellectually precocious; she excels at school, particularly in maths. Number two arrives, Louise or Lulu for short. She turns out to be a whirlwind character who refuses to eat infant formula and cries and claws violently every night. When Chua tries to sit her down at the piano, she smashes at the keys with her open palms. And so it goes on. According to Chua, the tiger mother, her second daughter inherited her own hot-tempered, viper-tongued, fast-forgiving personality while the eldest got the quiet, inquisitive qualities of her father.

Coming to the aspect of nurture: willingly or unwillingly, wittingly or unwittingly parents treat each child differently and thus stimulate a different development to take place. While they may never admit to it, many parents have a favourite child with whom they click more easily or in whom they recognize traits of their own. This has nothing to do with love. They might love all their children in equal measure and still connect with one more easily than with another out of a shared interest, a similar sense of humour or the same position in the birth order. When a son is born after you, your parents will attend to him differently than they did and do to you. The youngest ones have a status all their own. There's no need for them to grow up quickly. Let them remain the baby of the bunch, is the message they are being given, in overt and covert ways.

> *'You don't have to be famous. You just have to make your mother and father proud of you.'*
>
> —— MERYL STREEP on *Goodreads.com*

All in all the differences between siblings prove substantial. Even in identical twins who share one hundred per cent of their DNA, longitudinal studies have shown huge differences in personality. In their book *Separate lives: Why Siblings Are So Different*, published in 1990, developmental psychologists Judy Dunn and Robert Plomin present evidence for the substantial influence of the environment on character development. 'Despite the diversity of definitions of personality,' they write, 'a simple conclusion emerges from studies in this field: siblings are markedly different. The average sibling correlation for personality is only fifteen percent, which implies that about 85 percent of the variance of personality is not shared by two children growing up in the same family.' This means that each of us resembles our siblings only slightly more than we do the children of the neighbours or of people miles away whose children grow up in entirely different circumstances.

## No 2: the opposite

The previously mentioned Kevin Leman has his view on the salient dissimi-larities between siblings. Children grow up together. He is happy to wage a bet on a rule of thumb that he has seen proven over and over again in his private practice: the second child typically shoots off in a direction opposite to the firstborn. In general, one psychologist after another reports, the eldest child will usually identify with the parents, with whom they had exclusive time together at first. The eldest has learned the ropes, she knows the house rules and likes to uphold them. She may turn into a little policewoman who makes sure the others behave according to standards. She herself will set the example and when number two just falls in line, all is fine.

Number two, however, has a different interest at stake. The new kid on the block has to carve out their own place, which they will never achieve by carefully copying number one. That is the reason why the second one often opts for a strategy that is diametrically opposed: when the eldest is obedient and good because that makes her feel cherished and safe, the second-born will tend towards rebellion. This child will not meekly conform to how things are done, at home or at school. In the eyes of the first this is incredibly risky behaviour. Out of fright she will opt to act even more properly, which in turn evokes a more mischievous response from the second-born.

The Darwinists among the psychologists who study birth order see this as the only way for the second child to shape the triangle of the parents plus the eldest into a square in which they can occupy a corner of their own.

Imagine the little red beaks of baby birds, still without feathers, who stumble about the nest shivering. As soon as they notice one of their parents flying in with a titbit of food, they all open their beaks as wide they can in an effort to be the first to be fed, pushing each other out of the way. The Darwinists contend that in essence the same holds true for children of the human species. We all crave the full attention and affection of our parents. The biggest chance of receiving that is not by being the same but, on the contrary, by standing out. So when you as eldest daughter have chosen to secure your place in the family by being thoughtful, quiet and good, chances are that the one after you becomes an adventurous show-off. If you are the conventional kind, then the next one will like to venture into uncharted territory. When you as the eldest have taken on the role of leader, then number two can safely operate in your shadow and merrily walk through the doors that you have fought hard to open.

## A living doll

A new baby is also a playmate for the eldest, someone to be proud of and to embark on adventures with. Rufo signals a discrepancy between girls, who at age two or three have some sort of idea of what it means to be family, and boys, who in his view only find this out in adolescence. In his long career, Rufo, who is now over seventy years of age, has repeatedly seen girls help to take care of the baby – often as if it was a living doll – and who in doing so, in his interpretation, unwittingly did a trial run for when they would become mothers themselves.

In her *Memoirs of a Dutiful Daughter*, the influential French feminist author Simone de Beauvoir is very honest about her relationship to her younger sister. She would become cross, she writes, when her sister would disagree with her. Her sister would cry and they would make up. If her sister laughed at her jokes, Simone felt secure that she wasn't trying to humour her. Adults sometimes gave in to her, but her sister endowed her with authority – she obeyed her.

Another advantage is that with the two of you, you can do things that don't find favour with your parents. You stand stronger together and when punishment is meted out, you can both shrug your shoulders. You can exchange a look, fall about laughing and knock secret codes on the wall separating the bedrooms you are now each confined to. In the beginning, as the eldest you are the undisputed leader in every game being played. You put your little sister among the cuddly animals on the sofa because you are the teacher. You put your little brother up to badgering your mother to treat you to an ice-cream while you play innocent. At least, that's the plan. More often than not you are being told that you as the eldest ought to know better. You ought to be wiser. In the meantime, number two is growing fast. Steadily this child will try to over-take you left and right as they fight for their own rightful place in the family.

## Least loved

Reading the story from the vantage point of number two is special for an eldest daughter. Dr Jirina Prekop studied philosophy, psychology and peda-gogy. She was a student of the Nobel Prizewinner professor Nikolaas Tinber-gen, whose controversial holding therapy she expanded upon. This youngest daughter works from a perspective on family life in which punishments like a slap or dismissal are seen as fundamentally flawed. Not fear but love should, in her opinion, be the steering force in educating children. She has taught countless people how to solve conflicts by looking the other in the eye and continuing to allow your emotions to flow until you understand one another again. She has written fifteen books on the subject. Not bad for a second child from whom, as she perceived it, nothing much was expected.

As a child Jirina Prekop lived under the assumption that her parents did not love her as much as her sister, who was three and a half years older. Marus-ka was the undisputed star in the house, while she as a child had a hard time saying what she meant and resorted to stuffing herself with food. She felt like a second-class child. No wonder, she writes frankly in her book *Erstgeborene* (Firstborn), that she wasn't interested in doing anything along the same lines as her beautiful and clever eldest sister. Maruska remained in Prague her whole life where she became a medical doctor, married a reliable man and had two daughters of her own.

Although it had been her dream, Jirina did not go on to study medicine. In 1970, she fled her communist native country to move to Germany where she made a name for herself as a progressive psychologist and therapist. De-spite her deep familiarity with family patterns that had become her speciality, she only later developed an insight into the pain of the eldest who thinks it has forfeited the love of the parents when the second child is born.

When she started to talk about this with her own eldest sister, the resent-ment she had always felt started to dissipate. Only now did she hear how

Maruska had got the impression that all her mother wanted was to be occupied with the baby and how she had wanted to get back at her little sister by frightening her with tales of witches, letting her drink nasty concoctions and making her lie to their parents about this later. The sisters had grown apart, not merely because of the physical distance between them; by sharing how they had felt early on in their lives at home, reconciliation started to happen. 'Whatever has become of us,' Prekop writes, 'I honour her as my big sister and I take the place of the second in line. Maruska heaved an audible sigh of relief when I could tell her this. Mind you, we both were in our seventies!'

## Typical middle and youngest

The eldest daughter is not the only one ever to have felt dethroned. In the old days, families of eight or more were no exception and with every next birth, the former youngest was degraded to the position of a mere middle child. Many eldest daughters who come from such large families can write volumes about their role as second mothers. They had to help clean while the others were playing, or had to help cook for the whole bunch while their mother was busy feeding the youngest addition. Nowadays families tend to be much smaller; many younger eldest daughters have just one brother or sister. Whereas in the large families of past decades there used to be a ranking of the middle children – the youngest of the oldest ones or the eldest of the young cohort – many children nowadays are either simply the eldest or the youngest.

However, a number of second-born children also go through the experience of being dethroned. Almost one in five families still consists of more than two children. When number three announces itself, the second child in turn needs to get accustomed to the fact that the attention has to be shared with the newcomer. When parents have always known that they would like to have more children, they might already have treated the second one somewhat like a middle child, but there are second-borns who at the relatively late age of seven or ten are required to relinquish their role as youngest because another child has arrived somewhat unexpectedly. They don't always forgive the latecomer. Sometimes they keep reproaching the new youngest for many years because they have stolen their position. Objectively speaking, it is true that with each new birth, less time remains for the other kids as the cake has to be shared with more. For its part, the third child has to find a niche of its own in which it can claim a place in the pre-existing order – as does every next child.

By far the most arguments siblings have are about possessions. Young children already know exactly what is theirs. If a toy that belongs to someone else is taken from them, they will allow that to happen without much ado, but if it belongs to them, they will make sure they retrieve what is rightfully theirs. When the middle one has to fight the older child, who naturally is often bigger and stronger physically, then words are often a better weapon. It is also better not to attack the youngest one physically, as parents will generally not be pleased. Out of necessity, then, middle children may develop into diplomats who are able to come up with clever compromises. They are not dominant like the first or cute like the youngest. They teach themselves to listen carefully and be flexible and tolerant. They often grow into loyal, kind people. Personality tests reveal that middle children tend to get along amicably with most people.

Just as eldest children resemble one another, the youngest ones in a family are easily spotted: those spontaneous, socially adept, uncomplicated, humorous kid sisters and brothers. They were born in the spot that most people say they covet. It does look, from the outside, ideal – to be able to stay the baby of the family for ever and never need to be completely independent, because you know that with just the slightest helpless look someone will come running. Many allowances are made for the youngest, but there is a price to pay: the older children constantly monitor the little one. They are even known to counsel the parents in how to deal with the youngest.

*'We want everything to be perfect but nothing ever is. People don't have it all, I don't have it all. I think people get that.'*

— KYLIE MINOGUE in *The Daily Mail*

The life of the baby of the family seems at times not to have very clear boundaries. Anyone can just come in and tell them what to do. Not that the youngest is in the least perturbed by this; they know no different. Through their babyhood new faces appeared again and again over their crib, playpen or buggy. The whole family, of course, and probably also friends of the older children, fell in love with the new baby. That is the reason why many youngest children make friends easily – they tend to see strangers as friends they just happen not to have crossed paths with before.

The humour that many youngest children develop helps them in making new contacts. How do you make yourself heard when the others speak with much louder voices than yours on subjects that are beyond you? By being funny, of course. As a toddler you quickly learn to say something absurd and thus have everybody in stitches. You pull a silly face and before you know it, they're all looking at you. Youngest children are often irresistible clowns. Of course, when everyone laughs at the disarming baby of the family, the older children are at a loss – it is no small matter to get back parental attention.

In such scenarios, the eldest often becomes the stern one. 'Let's get serious,' her look seems to say; in this world life cannot be just about merrymaking. The table needs to be cleared. She is the first to get up and start doing the job – and many a time she is on her own. Her sense of care and duty are valued but not when things are just about to get fun.

## Not for the world

Not all eldest daughters are equally comfortable with the fact that they need to set the example – or think they need to set the example – for the rest of the siblings. Some of them give up before they get started. All those towering expectations are not for them. They are not going to be responsible and dutiful at all. They are not even going to try. They insubordinate, as it were, and refuse to serve. The books about birth order don't mention this category of eldest daughters who at a young age dig their heels in out of fear of failure. We heard quite a few stories, however, from second-born daughters who had taken the place of the eldest, who just could not get her life together.

After having obtained three master's degrees, because her elder sister always failed to finish any kind of education successfully, one of those second-born daughters has now vowed to take it easy. Or the woman who shared how her elder sister broke under the pressure of the high expectations on her; she developed anorexia and thus took herself out of the game. It was no surprise that this daughter had filled in for her. Now she is the hands-on, responsible one.

It would be interesting to know whether the eldest daughter's refusal of responsibility is apparent before the birth of the second child, or whether the dethronement by number two is the moment a number of eldest daughters give up, assuming they can never live up to the wishes of their parents and so they'd better not try at all. Let the other child, who is so suddenly the centre of attention, do the job. 'If they are so overjoyed with number two, then they had better take from him or her what I will never be able to give,' might be the toddler's reasoning. Either way, such an eldest daughter stops aiming to fulfil her parents' wishes whether they are real or just figments of her imagination. Here, Leman's rule of thumb applies again: the second child develops itself diametrically differently from the first and when the firstborn backs out the second daughter turns herself into a functional first.

Most eldest daughters, however, love being number one. They would not trade places with any one of their siblings for all the tea in China. Leave it to them to march on ahead, to get everyone organized, care for all and sundry and take the lead. 'If I believed in reincarnation, I would apply to be born as the eldest again next time round,' is how one eldest daughter expressed the general feeling during the Eldest Daughter Day.

## IN BRIEF

- With the second-born, parents are more realistic in their expectations, both of the child and of themselves.
- Every child must carve out its own place in which it gets its measure of attention.
- The second child develops diametrically differently from the first.

- The eldest may suffer from the feeling that it has lost the love of the mother to the new sibling.
- Middle children tend to be 'communicative mediators', whilst youngest charmers are often 'jesters'.
- Siblings only have a 15 per cent similarity; they resemble each other as little as they resemble the children next door.
- If the eldest does not claim responsibility, the daughter next in line will often develop into 'a functional eldest'.
- Many eldest daughters would never consider trading their place.

5.

# The big five characteristics

• • •

**WIES** What I wanted to do more than anything else was to write about fashion. Not as a reporter at fashion shows but as someone who looks at fashion as a reflection of what happens in the world. That prospect made my heart sing, but I dreaded telling anyone else. At the time I was in adult education; teaching Dutch was how I made my living.

One day, over dinner, a friend said to me: 'Why don't you just write something and send it to the newspaper you like best?' I said yes, I thought no, but in spite of my misgivings, in the end this is what I did.

I worked on this article for hours and hours. Would it satisfy the high demands of the editor? Was it critical enough, was it newsworthy? Friends had to read it and give me their feedback. My insecurity must have driven them crazy. Finally I sent it in, only to hear nothing back for a long, long time. Not for one moment during that endless time of waiting did the thought enter my mind: 'It will all be fine, it just takes time, the people on the editorial staff have more important things to do than read my text.' I was convinced that they did not like it. It would be binned straight away.

A few weeks later my piece was published. Even though I could hardly believe it, this encouraged me to continue. I wrote about the meaning of the stripes on Picasso's sweaters, about the tie of our prime minister and the feud between Yves St Laurent and Karl Lagerfeld. For just the national newspaper at first, then for an Amsterdam one, for a leading weekly and other popular magazines. When someone told me that I wouldn't want to write about something as superficial as fashion for the rest of my life, my stomach turned. See: not good enough, what

I did was not good enough. Still, I was driven to continue exploring this subject while at the same time being terrified of criticism and afraid to fall short. That they would call me and say: 'Wies, this story makes no sense at all.'

In the meantime, I earned my keep. I worked like mad. I loved it. I got to interview women like Jil Sander, an assignment for which the magazine flew me to Hamburg, Germany; had my own bimonthly column in a leading weekly; wrote articles about elder women who fell in love with men young enough to have been their sons, and so forth. Until I fell ill. I continued with some of my assignments but quite soon it became clear that it would be better for my health if I quit for a while. I thought a few weeks would suffice. Initially I saw this as a dramatic development in my life. It felt as if I would vanish from the face of the earth if I stopped working. Who was I if I didn't work? As the duration of my illness grew longer, these thoughts completely disappeared.

After two years of research it turned out I had ME – myalgic encephalomyelitis or chronic fatigue syndrome. This is named as a disease by the World Health Organization, but in the eyes of most doctors at that time it simply did not exist. It took me nine years to recover my health, and everything I had previously been doing with such diligence and zest was no longer on my mind. The little energy I had, I focused on getting better. Only when the English acupuncturist Mike Newland, the man who had dragged me through my disease, died unexpectedly did I feel the urge again to write and to be published. I started anew. First I wrote a book, my illness story, then I re-entered the workforce.

After my long period of illness and the wise lessons given to me by Mike, I had expected my inner critic to have died down. Alas, this voice is still there. I am better at silencing it, and I know my inner critic only wants to help by preventing me from getting hurt, but I still find it a big job to handle this part of myself.

## We resemble one another

Slowly, through our categorization, a clear picture starts to emerge. Our tables are by now covered with books that affirm what we see again and again in the stories eldest daughters tell us about themselves. When we asked the participants in the Eldest Daughter Day for the one word that characterizes their life, the former editor-in-chief of the most-read women's magazine in the Netherlands, who had come along with her eldest daughter and granddaughter, resolutely said 'Responsibility'. Instantly there was a buzz. Women laughed and called out their recognition. The next one, too, named responsibility as the principal quality of the birth position that we all shared. 'Holding everything together,' the third one said. Other suggestions came in: 'A strong sense of duty, being protective, taking the lead in organizing things, a bridge-builder, being groundbreaking, independent, innovative, thoughtful, strong, unpolished, a pioneer.' Taking all of this into account, we arrived at the following big five qualities that we see time and again as characteristic of eldest daughters:

1. responsible
2. dutiful
3. hands-on
4. thoughtful
5. caring

These five powerful qualities are all expressions of the one wish to continue to be allowed to belong. Many eldest daughters realized that the fear that they would be ejected from the nest explained their constant need to do everything right at all times. Everything. At all times. We recognize these traits in ourselves. We see them in one another. We find them in the studies that have been done on the subject. As eldest daughters we appear to have developed ourselves inevitably along the same lines. More even than our siblings, we resemble other women who are firstborns in their family. We resemble one another in the deep-rooted belief that we could safeguard our place by being good and performing well. We are alike in our conclusion that, as the eldest, we needed to uphold the rules of the house and had to take care of the rest. We are similar in our conviction that we are responsible. That if we don't do it...

## Thinking, feeling, acting

Simply sharing these qualities doesn't mean that as eldest daughters we are interchangeable. You recognize a snowflake as a snowflake, even though no two are the same. We all have our unique history, our own story. We have been born at different times, in different places on earth, in families with their own habits and rules. We also have different dispositions. For instance, when answering the question about the precise moment they realized they were eldest daughters, many women spoke of the responsibility they had continued to feel for their younger siblings when they themselves had already left home.

More than once, a conversation arose about how they had behaved when younger brothers or sisters came to them for help in a tense domestic situation. The way they responded to these major and minor crises is a good illustration of the three core dispositions we identified. One eldest daughter relayed how she had kept her cool when her younger brother and sister had shared their domestic hardships with her. She had listened attentively, asked a few questions for clarity and made an analysis of the various options for action. In her calm and collected way she had been a huge support for her younger siblings, who could not see the forest for the trees. With her level-headed advice, she is a good example of someone who approaches life mostly from the rational mind and thus comes to solutions that have been well thought through.

Another woman said that in a similar situation she had hugged her younger brother and sister close. Finally those two, who had faced a difficult situation at home so courageously, could let go for a while. In the presence of their eldest sister, they had been able to access their grief and let their tears flow. Together the three of them had come to the conclusion that while nothing much might change overnight in their domestic situation, at least they were together. The fact that the younger ones had been able to let off steam with their eldest sister was of great help. They felt she was there for them as an emotional support.

A third woman shared that she had promptly gone into action; when she was told about her younger siblings' domestic difficulties she had stood up for them immediately. Without losing so much as a second she had gone to her parents and had a fierce conversation with them. Her first impulse was not to get the facts straight or to shower her siblings with love, but to do, act, move and make things happen.

The domestic situations might not have been entirely the same but these three examples do convey the very different approaches stemming from the same basic sense of responsibility. Thinking, feeling or acting – one way is not better than the other, but it is interesting to reflect for a while on which modus operandi you favour, as each approach colours the big five characteristics that we as eldest daughters share.

## Responsible

If you could get a degree in responsibility, eldest daughters would no doubt qualify at a very young age. From childhood they are used to being held responsible. 'Will you hold him for a minute? Then I can open the door to Granny and Grandpa.' And later: 'Will you make sure she crosses the street safely? Well done. I know I can rely on you.' Or, 'Will you make sure the others dress warmly after your swim?' And, 'Stop quarrelling now. You're the oldest and the wisest.' There is no end to the examples of situations in which parents consciously or unconsciously delegate responsibility to their eldest.

When they are not given responsibility from someone else, then eldest children are apt to take it upon themselves. 'I will spoon-feed her, Mum. You go and do your work,' an eldest daughter says as if she were a colleague. In the schoolyard she keeps an eye out for her younger siblings and moves in when they are being harassed. Whoever troubles her brothers and sisters will have to deal with her. She is responsible for their well-being after all.

As a result, many eldest daughters become masters at feeling responsible for all and sundry. For what their child or colleagues say to others, for how others think about them, for the neighbour's cat that is meowing on the balcony in the dark of night, for climate change. You name it, an eldest daughter will be able to feel personally responsible for it. That's why it came as no surprise to us that, when asked what is significant in their life, many eldest daughters named their big sense of responsibility first. Since time immemorial they have been functioning as an example to others. The children that came later looked up to them and imitated their behaviour – or protested against that responsible goody-two-shoes eldest sister leading the pack. Whichever way, the responsibility that many eldest daughters unconsciously adopted only grew.

Eldest daughters achieve a lot with this sense of responsibility. They develop themselves into multitaskers who can handle a lot. They are good to have around or in a team, these responsible types, but a look into their heart shows that they would love to be able to switch off this sense of being responsible for each and every person from time to time. A human being just cannot be held responsible for everything. And you can also go too far. Younger sisters have been known to cry out in frustration, 'When will you finally allow me to lead my own life?' Their eldest sister will often be taken aback. That is so not what she meant. She only wanted to help. She had no idea that her sense of responsibility could be oppressive.

You may feel responsible for the relationships that you have with people, for the way you spend your time and how you treat others, as well as for your own happiness. Keeping an eye on that prevents you committing to others until the point of exhaustion, until you come to your own limitations or those of the people involved. The issue at hand is to learn to trust that people can manage without you. To accept that upon reading that last sentence you think that yes, they might manage but that you would have done things just a bit better, and to hold back in spite of that.

## Dutiful

The five of us who comprised the organizing team of the Eldest Daughter Day had three meetings. That was all it took as each one of us sent what they had promised to progress to the others well in advance. Of course, this was not just an update but a constructive next iteration. There is a paradox here. As the authors, we were the ones taking the initiative for this day; and both of us find it no less than normal always to have everything we said we'd do finished and well-presented ahead of time. Yet, we had not expected the dedication and commitment to the project of the other eldest daughters we involved in the preparations for our research day. That surprise gave us a good idea of the work ethos that numerous eldest daughters apply: whatever I do, I will do well. The deeper we went into our enquiry, the more clearly we saw this attitude confirmed.

Eldest daughters are dutiful, even when no one else is looking. The house needs to be kept tidy, the work finished, all done and dusted for tomorrow. No inspector will come and check. They themselves are the inspectors. If they paid attention, they would hear a sigh of relief every time they offer to do a job. Everyone knows that the task will be done well – on time and to high standards. Sometimes eldest daughters would love to be released from the perennial sense of duty. How often have they told themselves, 'Today I will not volunteer for anything. I'll sit back quietly and wait until someone steps forward'? But then the project deadline approaches and no one seems to be too worried about it, except for the dutiful eldest daughter. 'OK,' she will hear herself say again, 'I'll do it.' Whether this is at home or at work, at the children's sports club, in a group of friends or serving on a board. Wherever she is, she'll do what's needed and do it well.

Obeying a sense of duty is a wonderful quality. But the one who agrees too fast or thinks too often, 'Yes, just leave it to me,' ends up with such a long to-do-list that there will never be an end to it. The occasional refusal will not harm a soul. No one will be surprised; they will just go to the next person or they will face up to the task themselves. We're not saying it is easy to say no. Even just entertaining that option will start a voice in your head saying that soon no one will ask you for anything. These are the thoughts of the young child that wanted to make itself indispensable. That way it would earn its right to keep belonging within this family that all of a sudden had expanded. When you want to leave the treadmill of commitments and wish to be able to make a free choice, you'll realize where the inner voices come from and resist the whirlwind of thoughts that tell you the world will end if you are not involved. This is the time to pluck up your courage and ignore the voices within. When you don't succeed in saying 'no' right away, saying 'yes' less frequently might be the way to go. Indicate your boundaries and stick to them, agree on who is taking over doing the shopping from you, who will go and take a walk with your old mother or close the office as the last one out. Anyone who wants to change things will have to stand their ground. It is worthwhile to do so. The woman who feels as free to say 'no' as to say 'yes' takes fate in her own hands. That way being dutiful can remain a powerful quality to have.

## Hands-on

Many eldest daughters have a natural overview and organizational skills. They come in the door, see what needs to happen and distribute the tasks. Piece of cake. Others often agree without complaints or questioning. They do what the eldest thinks fit. They acknowledge the obvious authority, even if the eldest in many cases is completely oblivious to the fact that to others she looks every inch a leader. She just does as she has always done. It goes without saying that it is up to her to take the initiative. Who else could?

With good humour some call themselves an incredible – or even a professional – meddler. They like to poke their noses into other people's affairs and before they know it, they have been given the management of a project or been asked to sit on the board. Often, people are especially delighted with her decisive action. Her overview, her foresight and her practical, hands-on attitude – they like to be led by someone like this.

In his workshops for teachers, Kevin Leman approaches the influence of birth order position in the family home in a direct way. He asks the attendees to form four groups: only children, firstborns, middle-borns and last-borns. He then asks them to chat about their experiences and qualities they might share. The only children and firstborns waste no time in entering into serious conversations, while the middle-born and last-born groups usually stand around chatting about anything and everything.

As inconspicuously as possible he walks around and leaves a sheet of paper face down in the centre of each group. The pieces of paper all contain identical instructions: 'Congratulations! You are the leader of this group. Make sure that you are ready to report to the others on the personality characteristics that you all seem to share within fifteen minutes.'

As he writes in his renowned 1985 *The Birth Order Book*, almost invariably a person in the only or firstborn group picks up the paper and reads the instruction. Someone from the middle-born or last-born groups grabs the piece of paper first, according to Leman, as often as it snows in Ibiza. The middle-borns might follow suit but the youngest are often having such a good time that they are completely oblivious to what is happening around them. The firstborns and only children give a good presentation to the rest of the group, the middle-borns sometimes do and sometimes don't. The last-borns use all their charm to state their innocence. Someone ought to have told them what to do! Of course this has everybody laughing as they all see how they themselves and the others are true to type: the eldests waste no time being efficient – they see what needs to be done and resolutely do it – while the last-borns fool around and wait until someone reminds them of the task at hand. In this way, Leman gives teachers an experience of the difference between the children in their classrooms.

Of course, disposition and temperament also have their parts to play. One child may be shy and inclined to hold back, while the other is more of a show-off. In areas where the eldest feels safe, she will naturally take the initiative, make up a game and be the leader. Later these expeditious girls grow into adults who are able to take decisions when push comes to shove – for an eldest that is as natural as sunshine in the Sahara. It is a quality that takes them into leading positions, in both smaller and larger contexts. The eldest daughter takes the lead. And what she has in mind is how it will be.

## Thoughtful

Time and time again, research on schoolchildren shows that firstborns like to go to school and spend more years studying than later-borns. This is not because they need to take classes twice. Quite the contrary. They want to know what makes the world tick and thus love to spend more time finding out. They are the interested ones who sit in the front row, the bookworms who always do their homework, the scholars who can always find something new to explore. Many researchers attribute this studious attitude to the fact that the parents usually have unrealistically high expectations of their first child and take everything she does extremely seriously. They tend to be much more relaxed with the other children from the start; when a later-born first mumbles their own name, it is not celebrated as something worthy of the evening news. The first one, however, is closely watched and permanently scrutinized. Is she not slow in her development, why can she not handle a knife and fork yet, does she score well at school and what is this thing with this boy who is hanging around all the time? Each step is given so much thought that you cannot help but become rather thoughtful yourself.

The eldest daughters we spoke to in the course of our research, too, indicated that they had preferred going to school to having free time. What to do with that time that you could also have applied to something useful? They liked being at school. There they met their friends and learned about the world outside of wherever they happened to grow up. And if you could have seen how they applied themselves to answering our questions, diving into their memories and telling their stories at the Eldest Daughter Day, then you would agree with us: they took themselves and our research incredibly seriously. The youngest sons who supported us on the technical side were stunned. Were they ever to work on a similar day about the lives of last-borns, it would be much more chaotic, that they knew for sure.

Let's be honest, eldest daughters are generally not the court jesters. If other siblings clear the air at a painful moment by cracking a joke, the eldest may rather find herself inclined to remain quite grave. Let's have a good conversation here, is what she thinks. And yes, she would love to be able to take life a little less seriously at times, but she wouldn't really know how. Wordplay may be her forte, as eldests are often exceptionally good at languages, probably as a result of being alone with their parents for the early part of their lives.

There are many advantages to coming at life from a place of being astute and thoughtful. Eldest daughters dig deep, do their homework and come well-prepared. That is why they shine in occupations that require precision and meticulousness. Accountancy, law and the medical profession, for instance. They become architects or apothecaries, teachers, office managers, supervisors or their own bosses. They are often gifted organizers. They keep the overview while also having a keen eye for detail.

If they are given an assignment, then they tend to think that they need to know everything about the subject before being able to say anything. At times this is a handicap because the article has a deadline, the sentence must be passed at a given point or the design has to be finished so it can be presented. In this way you'll have to learn to live with what you cannot do and trust that with your conscientious approach you won't fail to deliver the quality that is required. If you do receive a word of criticism one day, it is not the end of the world – even if you will probably consider moving to Alaska immediately. You already knew that your work was not up to par and so most of all you feel caught out. In this case, it is no use becoming even more meticulous. By becoming more aware of your serious approach you might be able to relax more. Accept that, like everyone else and in spite of your best efforts, you sometimes make mistakes. Just breathe deep and merrily carry on.

## Caring

It is wonderful to take care of others. It gives satisfaction. Brewing tea for someone who is sad, pressing fresh juice for a child who is not feeling well, offering help and advice to a friend in trouble. You settle in and pretend you have all the time in the world. You feel that this is what the other person needs at such times: someone who really listens, who wants to do something for you, be there for you. As an eldest, for you this is no trouble at all. It does not feel like a burden to lavish your time and attention on others. To arrange something for them that they are unable to or step in when it makes someone happy.

When young, eldest daughters often act as a bridge between the parents and the younger children. You watched your parents and saw how much they appreciated you taking care of the youngest so they were able to have a quiet conversation together. You motioned your younger siblings out of the way when your mother took a rest and made her tea upon waking. You made sure you got good marks at school so your parents at least need not worry about you.

During the Second World War, one eldest daughter said at the Eldest Daughter Day, she put her own life in danger for her younger sister. She still thinks it is obvious why she did this at the time. She was the eldest, wasn't she, so it was up to her to protect her younger sibling. Some copy the caring ways of their mothers, like eldest daughter Beyoncé. 'If I weren't performing, I'd be a beauty editor,' she says, 'or a therapist. I love creativity, but I also love to help others. My mother was a hairstylist and they listen to everyone's problems – like a beauty therapist!'

Once you have an eye for what others need or what makes them happy, you never lose it. Just like you did when you were small, you will be apt to look around wherever you are. Is everyone happy? Are things going well here? What can I do to make things even better? Taking care of others, whether at home or at work, has its limits. You cannot run around after others for ever – but at the same time there is no end to the amount one could do. There is always another lonely soul out there who you could visit, or a colleague who is suffering hardship and would be only too glad to unburden to someone with a listening ear. It is not hard to be fully occupied with family, friends, colleagues and acquaintances in need of tender loving care. But in the meantime, who takes care of you?

When do you as an eldest daughter feel welcome, satisfied and worthy? Could it be that you believe that you only matter when you take care of everyone else? When you continually lend a helping hand to people around you and save the world while you're at it? This raises the question: do you allow others to take care of you? With whom can you blow off steam and who lends you a shoulder to rest your head? An eldest daughter tends to be better at caring for others than at caring for herself. I'll manage, is the image you usually project. Yes, you are strong. You can handle a lot. But even your large reservoir of care and love may get exhausted at some point. It may help not to hide it when you are at the end of your tether. Do not pretend that you are invulnerable. Of course it is scary to let people in on the secret that there are times when your plate is too full and you need some care. It takes practice. You may want to start with something so small that no one will notice. For once just accept when a friend, seeing that you are dead tired, offers to cook you a meal. Don't begrudge her the opportunity to have this wonderful feeling one gets from caring for someone else.

## THE BIG FIVE AT A GLANCE

These are the five core qualities that we as eldest daughters have developed.

## RESPONSIBLE

The quality most eldest daughters name first is their big sense of responsibility. It has helped you achieve great things. You would like to be able to switch it off from time to time but have no clue how. You feel responsible for the well-being of all and the happy endings of everything. You are not always aware of the boundaries of your responsibility. This has you beavering away until you come to your own boundary – often the point of exhaustion. You must learn to let go. Trust that people can manage successfully without you.

## DUTIFUL

When you take something on, others breathe a sigh of relief for they know that they can count on you. Whatever you do is done to perfection, whether it is upholding family traditions or organizing a research day at work. You may want to put your sense of duty on the back burner at times; but each time you deliver a project on time, you also feel the satisfaction of being someone others can rely on.

### HANDS-ON

You come in the door, see what needs to happen and distribute the tasks. Easy. As a matter of course others do what the eldest thinks fit. They acknowledge your self-evident authority, even if you are not aware that they are perceiving this. Some might consider you a busybody but often people are pleased with the way you take things in hand – with your overview, your foresight and efficiency, they like to be led by you. And yes, they do think you are on the bossy side, while you have no clue whatsoever that this is the image you project.

### THOUGHTFUL

Let's be honest: a court jester you will never be. You tend to look at life from a place of being serious and thoughtful. There is a lot to see there. You know much about the background of both issues and people. In conversations you will prefer the route of enquiry to superficiality. People may find you ponderous at times, but you just love digging deeper. Friends appreciate this trait as they find you an interesting person to talk to, and a good listener. And ten to one you have found a profession where your thoughtful side is an advantage.

### CARING

When all are satisfied and happy, so are you. And it is up to you to make sure that happens. Your care can range from that of dear ones close to you to people in dire straits around the world. You would love to be able to 'make it up to' them. Maybe you keep it small and are available to the people around you at all times – they can always come to you with their worries. Or perhaps you express your caring side by campaigning to change the overarching systems that perpetuate injustice. A snag is that you tend to forget to care for yourself.

# 6

# I need to be perfect

...

**WIES** It was an immense drawing of a pink smiling Buddha. I had laboured for days to get it all exactly right. The finger pointing upwards, the folds in his belly and, strangely enough, I also remember big gold loops in his ears. To get the gold colour just right required an effort. Not that I was such a star with paint and brushes, but this assignment, from our art teacher at high school, had apparently inspired me. I can still see the final result in my mind's eye. I was happy. The teacher was not. That is to say, he gave me a seven out of ten. A seven! For something I myself thought was perfect. I had expected a much higher mark. This hit home. If I wanted to aim for perfection, I had better not do any more drawings, must have been my conclusion at the time.

This event happened when I was about fourteen. Many years later when I studied Dutch at university, I let myself be persuaded by a friend to take a pottery class at the cultural centre for students. Now I have to tell you that this friend later went to art school as she had, as they say, 'the eye'. I allowed myself to be persuaded, thinking I had to try something new in that area after all those years, even if only for fun. Messing around with clay seemed a useful therapeutic break from spending my days absorbed in books.

So I donned an apron and stood next to my friend, who wholeheartedly gave herself up to claying the head of the model. After only fifteen minutes I could clearly make out the nose of the woman posing in front of us in the statue she was fashioning. I did my best to suppress the thought that I had better stop because I would never be a brilliant sculptor anyway, and went to work. Half an hour later the teacher passed by. She explained how the successful pieces would be stored to dry while the lesser objects would be thrown back into the big pile of clay on the floor to be used again. Guess where my artwork ended up... My friend tried to placate me by saying that at least I had been totally engrossed in this pleasant activity for over an hour. Alas, the harm had already been done. I did accompany her to this class twice more, but then I quit for good. Being engaged in an activity that I know I will never excel in and doing so just for fun – well, no, that is just not me.

Of course I know that it is valuable to enjoy the moment when you are engaged in any kind of creative expression. Or to quote an ancient Chinese wisdom: the road is the destination. When I fill in answers to the questions on perfectionism that follow in this chapter, my score is high. I can devour endless psychologists' books, visit healers and meditate, but the urge to perform well is not easily overcome. This requires practice and patience, a lot of patience.

## Free choice

Many eldest daughters feel that the behaviour that stems from the five big characteristics is the most natural thing in the world. It doesn't occur to them that they could be different. They do not identify the sense of responsibility they feel for the rest of their family as a trait typical of eldest daughters. They don't regard their diligence, to make sure everything and everyone is well, as part of their history as a firstborn. This is just the way they do things. They often are 'unconsciously competent', as the phrase goes. Utterly proficient, incredibly capable – but because they are not aware of it, it's as if they don't realize that they have a choice.

> 'I try my best to be self-assured and look the part but at the same time just like any other woman I am not always thrilled with what the mirror reflects back to me in the morning. There is always something that should be different or better.'
>
> — DOUTZEN KROES on *elisabethcarrie.blogspot.nl*

Even when you start to realize that you would like to be a little less thoughtful at times and would even love occasionally to leave things as they are, you may find that it is easier said than done. It's hard to change overnight an attitude that you have unconsciously cultivated over long years of habit. You can, however, begin to adjust gradually as you become more aware of the way in which you lead your life. You may start to wonder one day if it is truly up to you to organize the family outing as you have done so often before – or whether your agenda is full and someone else could have a go at it. Do you really need to be the one who makes sure that everyone feels happy? Somewhere inside there is this voice that tells you to excel at everything you do and preferably be the best in the field, but how can you tell when you are? When are you good enough? Perpetually asking questions like this can drive you crazy. Handbooks that describe the way to measure your 'enoughness' have not been written, councils that determine what is in and out of the bounds of what is achievable don't exist, nor do officials who can state with authority how the matter stands.

You are the one who has the final say, but eldest daughters are known to let their ambition to excel in several fields simultaneously take them for a ride. Especially in circumstances when one or both parents were quick to criticize, chances are that the eldest will constantly try to meet with her parents' approval and will not rest until she feels she is achieving perfection, even if she has become a grown woman who is making a successful career. The voice that propelled her as a child is still guiding her actions. She wants to be a good mother as well as have a high-flying job, be the perfect partner for the love of her life as well as a trusted friend whose door is always open. After all, we live in a time in which a woman can be active on many fronts.

When as an eldest daughter you want all of that, it is likely that you will run into a sneaky phenomenon, i.e. the treacherous tendency towards perfectionism. In that case the benchmark, which in the eyes of others you have already set sky-high, never satisfies you. As soon as you have achieved one goal, you see another on the horizon. Whatever you accomplished yesterday doesn't really count. That is done and dusted, and it was not a big deal to begin with as far as you're concerned. You're not one to look back and take pride in what you've built, let alone relax for a moment. The only thing that counts, your deceptive thoughts tell you, is what needs doing today. Or rather, what has to be done *well* today, preferably to perfection.

### ARE YOU A PERFECTIONIST?

Do you call yourself a perfectionist or are you under the impression that this doesn't apply to you? To be sure you could ask yourself a number of questions. Perfectionists come in all shapes and sizes. You could be a serious case – someone who becomes completely paralyzed and doesn't do anything because the perfect is out of reach – or you could be someone who suffers less, while still finding that it gets in the way. Should you recognize yourself in only a few of the descriptions below, don't stop reading.

### MOOD SWINGS

Your mood is fully dependent upon your latest success or mistake. When someone pays you a compliment for your work you are elated; when someone disapproves in the slightest of part of your work, you are downcast. You think you will never amount to anything.

### THE MORE, THE BETTER

You want to do and experience as many things as possible in your life. The result can't always be great, but quantity is more important than quality.

### TELESCOPIC THINKING

When you think of the things on your to-do list, it feels as if you are looking through a telescope: they appear much bigger than they are. The opposite also holds true; when you look at everything you have done in the past, your accomplishments seem rather insignificant.

## FOCUS ON THE FUTURE

You have done something exceptionally well – so what? You really cannot take time out to congratulate yourself and enjoy the moment. You are already fully occupied with the next project. You need to get on with it. Forever onward.

## WORRYING ABOUT THE PAST

When you are not worrying about the future, you are considering mistakes you have made in the past. You wonder why you haven't gone about things better. You play the 'what-if game' with yourself. 'What would have happened if I had studied my heart's desire?'

## THE GOAL MUST BE REACHED

Of course you will relax once the goal is reached. Then you will have plenty of time to spend with your family – but first aims need to be met. While it may, obviously, be important to focus completely on a project at hand, the ultimate perfectionist keeps on going from one goal to the next at the expense of downtime for her family or for herself.

## PERFORMING WELL

You want to work at something until it is totally and truly perfect. The eternal question, however, is: when will that be? Are you ever satisfied or do you tend to find fault and keep at it? Do you ever live up to your own expectations or is the work never really finished as far as you are concerned?

## ALL OR NOTHING THINKING

You are not content until you are the best in everything you take on. You may have raised the nicest children, have a glittering career and on top of that organize the most convivial dinner parties for your friends, but if for example you are not asked to take part in a project and your colleague is, all of a sudden – in your own eyes – you are the ultimate failure.

## Brave and imperfect

Descriptions of people who are perfectionists tend to be rather dramatic. They are people, the stories go, who aim for the impossible, who want to have everything organized perfectly at all times, even in their social life, who are neurotic in getting their desk, their kitchen and their whole house in order, who cannot sleep if the washing has not been folded, if tomorrow's outfit is not laid out, or if the administration from the previous quarter is not finished straight away. They are the ones who have a super-critical eye out for themselves and others, who can always find fault or see how things could have been done better. They are averse to leaving tasks to someone else, even if in their heart they are aware that delegation is the name of the game, but it is just so hard when you are convinced you can do the job better than anyone else.

Another aspect of perfectionists is that they will apologize deeply once they get the impression that they haven't performed well, or well enough. In extreme cases perfectionists don't expect ever to be successful and so they don't even get started on a project. The sheer prospect of being found lacking stops them in their tracks. Hence their high expectations become a self-fulfilling prophecy because by not getting started they find themselves lacking, even if they may cherish the illusion that one day, one fine day they will have things organized in such a way that their dream project will come true precisely as they had always thought it would. Real perfectionists often think in terms of black and white. They are highly opinionated on what people should and should not do and in voicing these opinions they don't spare themselves.

*'I am not perfect at all. I make high demands of myself but whether that is a good quality to have...'*

— GWYNETH PALTROW in *Vogue*

Being a perfectionist is no picnic. Do we as eldest daughters have traces of this affliction? In many cases the answer is 'yes', even though there are of course nuances. Not everyone suffers from it in the extreme measure described above, but many of us firstborns cooked up the idea that we were going to do our best to become top of the bill, and if that proved to be insufficient to ensure our place in the sun we would just try harder. This approach seemed to be the only way to justify our right to exist. Only by avoiding making any mistakes whatsoever and by getting things perfect, we think, do we stay in control of our lives.

A consequence of this line of reasoning might be that you turn into a largely inflexible person, averse to change. If something goes well, you will want to keep it exactly the way it is – until the moment you discover that it is fine to strive for perfection, but that, equally, you are not a lesser person when things go wrong. Finally then you are getting somewhere. It is then that you break the spell the drive towards perfection casts. Enlightened, you may realize that people close to you don't judge you by how well you perform. They already love you and they will not stop doing so. Even if it is a drag when the report you wrote is rejected or when you let the apple cake burn. You'll have to make do. No one likes to come up short but this has nothing to do with who you are. You are good, even without being the perfect manager, mother or nurse, and you will not be thrown out of the nest.

What you can do is try to excel in what you do without getting tied up in the idea that you have to be perfect, and that you will amount to nothing if you are not. You seek to perform as well as you can because you have set yourself certain aims in life. You have an intention and want to live accordingly. It takes courage to pursue this course and not be afraid of what is imperfect. The truth is that as human beings we can never attain perfection. Tackling tasks as best you can on the basis of wanting to help others or creating a better world is a great quality. It will teach you that perfect does not exist, that you make mistakes like everybody else and that you may always try to be perfect in everything you do, without ever expecting to be so. In the words of J.K. Rowling, who is an eldest daughter and also has one, 'The knowledge that you have emerged wiser and stronger from setbacks means that you are, ever after, secure in your ability to survive.'

In essence, the antidote to perfectionism is to be kind to yourself when with the best of intentions you do what you always did; to allow yourself the liberty to stumble, to slide and fall and just get up again.

## The benefits of failure

Watching other perfectionists at work will show you how disheartening a drive for perfection can be for others. Who is not familiar with an eldest daughter who is a top achiever but still continues to push herself until she collapses? Her exhaustion can also be turned into a drama as she may start to think, 'See! I am no good, I get it all wrong all the time. My whole life is a failure.'

> *'It's obviously nerve-racking, because I don't know the ropes really. William is obviously used to it, but I'm willing to learn quickly and work hard.'*
>
> — KATE MIDDLETON, now the Duchess of Cambridge, on *ITV News*

Robbert Dijkgraaf is director of the prestigious Institute for Advanced Study in Princeton, New Jersey. In an interview he once said that to his disappointment many teachers don't conduct experiments in their physics classes out of fear that they will fail. This is typical of the kind of education most of us have received at school: we are supposed to avoid making mistakes, even though mistakes can be excellent teaching tools and also at times produce unexpected discoveries. 'Making mistakes is the best way I know to learn and improve your performance', says this mathematical physicist, who has made significant contributions to string theory and the advancement of science education.

The creator of Harry Potter and his world has addressed the benefits of failure on several occasions. In her witty 2008 Harvard commencement speech, J.K. Rowling, said: 'It is impossible to live without failing at something, unless you live so cautiously that you might as well not have lived at all

– in which case, you fail by default.' She was speaking from experience; after her marriage imploded, she found herself a lone parent without a job, and as poor as it is possible to be in modern Britain without being homeless. She felt a complete and utter failure, but to her amazement the upside was that everything that was not essential was stripped away. 'I was set free, because my greatest fear had been realized. I was rock bottom, but I was still alive, I still had a daughter whom I adored, and I had an old typewriter and a big idea. I stopped pretending to myself that I was anything other than what I was, and began to direct all my energy into finishing the only work that mattered to me.' We all know what that yielded.

So it is clear then. Just strive for the best, don't cry too hard when things go pear-shaped and specifically don't keep thinking you've blundered once again. No day goes by that doesn't provide you with the opportunity to practise improving yourself without wanting to be perfect and better than the rest. The first step is to be aware of why you are doing something, the second is to intervene when your underlying motivation is off; but above all: accept who you are.

## Daring to be vulnerable

Dr Brené Brown, a research professor at the University of Houston Graduate College of Social Work, is well-known worldwide as an expert in this field. Her TED Talk about the power of vulnerability is one of the top ten most-watched clips on that site. She attributes its popularity to the fact that she did not choose her 'old friends security and control' to guide her and present what would probably have been a good talk; instead she chose to own up to the vulnerability that she had been researching all those years through the stories of others.

The next day she had, as she says, the worst vulnerability hangover of her life. She felt she had exposed herself too much to the audience and the cameras, and shame hit her like a tidal wave. At what point had she thought it would be a good idea to talk openly about her breakdown, she wondered in her despair. She had to move somewhere else, was her conclusion in this state of overpowering panic. Leave town. Flee the inevitable public shaming for which she had no one to blame but herself. The thing was, she had nowhere to go. She has lived in Texas her whole life, she has a great job at the university, her children go to the local school.

When the inner storm died down, her fear, of course, proved completely ungrounded. To the contrary, her courage to have not pretended to be the perfect researcher but instead tell a personal story had touched people deeply. This only confirmed what she found in the numerous interviews she held to gather data for the Grounded Theory approach that we also used as the basis for this book, and which forms the basis of her theory: we are afraid to be vulnerable but when we gather enough courage to show ourselves as we are, that is when the true connection that we crave happens.

Brown is the eldest of four. What she as an eldest daughter, as a passionate researcher, as a woman of this age, has had to learn is to have compassion for herself. Or in plain English: to be kind to herself and accept herself fully as she is, with all her talents and weaknesses. This is what her research into connection required her to do: to stay connected herself. Over and over she has had to face her own fears: that people would think her crazy, that she would not belong, that she was not good enough. Just like all of us, time and again she is confronted with this choice: to be a good girl and take the conventional approach or to gather the courage to be open and show yourself in all your imperfection, to really make the connection with the other person and take a surprising next step together.

## IN BRIEF

- Perfectionism leads to lying awake at night and a perpetual wondering as to whether you are good enough.
- Eldest daughters often have no idea how much of a perfectionist they are.
- You can only choose freely when you are aware of the behaviour that stems from being the eldest.
- Discovery comes from making mistakes. You can pretend to be perfect or you can show your true self.
- True connection comes when you find the courage to be yourself, accepting what you are and are not able to do.

# 7.

# Friends for life

• • •

**LISETTE**  A dinner party with men only. That to me seemed the best way to celebrate my fiftieth birthday. All the men in my life gathered around a big table, and I seated among them like a princess. The only catch was that I thought it was a strange way to mark this milestone. When I mentioned this idea to my partner, as usual his advice was: 'You have to do what pleases you.' So it came to pass that I had a house full of men on a Friday night. The youngest was my nephew Thomas, with whom I have conducted conversations on all kinds of topics practically since the day he could speak; the oldest one present was my father. In between were old friends from my student days and men I had met through work or my female friends. They numbered nineteen. I introduced them to each other by saying why each of them was important to me: the ongoing conversation on spiritual topics with my friend Thomas; that in case of emergency I would use my last quarter to call my friend Lex; my gratitude to Eckart for seeing my potential; the steadfastness of Jos who loves me while seeing all of me.

In the weeks leading up to this big day I had given my relationships with these men a lot of thought. Why did they mean so much to me? Could it be that I projected my focus on my father onto them? That is highly probable. Also, I love talking about emotional issues with men while I have a bit of an issue doing this with my female friends. I must confess to a certain fear of the sharp tongue that women can have. Also, to be honest, I often feel the lesser one in the company of women, which I seldom do when in the company of men. I have no children to talk about and I am not well-versed in the kinds of friendly conversations many women delight in.

My women friends, however, did not take my birthday plan lying down. Three of them – all eldest daughters, of course, Wies being one of them – organized a surprise party with my female friends. They made me feel that even though I may often give work priority over a call or a meal together, and although I may give precedence to the company of men, they know they also play an essential role in my life.

When my sixtieth birthday came up I noticed I did want to celebrate with my female friends. My life had taken an undeniable turn towards the spiritual and I longed to share some of that with them. For weeks I went back and forth. I love my women friends and I am sure they love me, too, and yet I harbour certain fears. I do not want to burden them. I do not want to claim time in their busy lives. When I said this to one of them, she shook her head pityingly. How could I even think along those lines? So we got together on a Sunday. When I addressed each of them, tears started to flow. We have been through a lot in all the years of our friendship, and at this age there is so much going on in our own lives and the lives of people we love.

The afternoon with my girlfriends was precious. I am still not one to phone my friends very regularly and I still often opt to work instead of paying a visit to have a chat, but I do think of my women friends on a regular basis. Just like I think of the men in my life. I am grateful to all of them.

## Behind you

Singer and eldest daughter Carole King once voiced it so poetically in her song, *'You've Got a Friend'*, (from her album *Tapestry*, 1971):

> *You just call out my name*
> *And you know wherever I am*
> *I'll come running, to see you again.*

*Winter, spring, summer or fall*
*all ya have to do is call*
*and I'll be there, yes, I will*
*You've got a friend.*

King voices a feeling that many of us will recognize when trying to describe our image of friendship. A friend is someone who can call us in the middle of the night. You jump straight out of bed, gladly and without a moment's hesitation. Your support is needed and you're on your way. This is reciprocal. Friends are ready to help, especially at times when life is challenging and hard; they are there for you. They comfort, stimulate and admire you. They are behind you every step of the way, unconditionally. You also celebrate life together. Graduations, weddings, anniversaries, birthdays, book launches, holidays – life is better when shared with friends and when times are tough you try to lighten things up for each other. A life without friends is unimaginable – regardless of the number of friends you have, which obviously varies from person to person. Unlike your family, friends are people you have chosen yourself.

What kind of friends are eldest daughters? Going by the books by Leman and Richardson mentioned earlier, we are not the easiest people in the world to befriend. We do not fit in the category of people who have found four new friends within minutes of entering a room. We move slowly and carefully, taking our time to see which way the cat jumps, looking for a true connection that may require some time to mature. It may also be true that our traits of thoughtfulness, sense of duty and hands-on leadership prevent people from making easy contact with us. We can appear intense, with our desire to dive head first into a serious conversation with someone we have only just met. We might scare people off when we jump up too quickly to solve a problem, give our opinion and take the lead. Let's face it, we have a tendency to be patronizing. We are also fond of looking at subjects from all angles with our analytic mind, which may tire people out if they were just looking for a fun and friendly conversation. After all, friendship also exists in just sharing a meal and enjoying the beauty of the sunset.

*'Like most of us, I'm used to juggling about 52 roles in life. Wife. Mother. Sister. Friend. Author. Sometimes I feel a bit "multiple-personality'.*

— SOPHIE KINSELLA, on *MailOnline*

OK, so we possess a number of traits that in the first instance might get in the way of making friends easily, but once the deal is done in all probability we will be friends for life. Even if every phase of life brings new people with it, many firstborns maintain friendships from way back when. It has also been said that we will in all likelihood feel more at home with friends who are either a bit older or a bit younger than we are, and not so much with people our own age. Of course, this harks back to our younger years when as an only child we mainly associated with adults and later, after we had become the eldest, with children who were younger. This is an interesting fact to check with yourself. How old are your friends? Does your circle of friends display a colourful mixture of ages, as Dr Leman predicts?

## Birds of a feather

Do eldest daughters seek each other out as friends? Lisette and Wies discovered that many of their women friends turned out to be eldest daughters themselves. During the Eldest Daughter Day we asked participants to indicate the birth position of their best friend. Forty-three of the seventy-five women who ticked the box indicated that their bosom friend was indeed an eldest, while twenty-two said it was a youngest who is closest to their hearts and ten had a middle child for their best friend. If over half of the participants interviewed indicate that they have an eldest as their best friend, can this be considered just a coincidence?

The idea that birds of a feather find each other in friendship is affirmed by author and journalist A.C. Grayling in his book *Friendship*. Grayling conducted a deep study into what we define as friendship today and how this has evolved through the ages. According to him we instinctively apprehend that shared interests, a similar outlook on life, the same sense of humour and a comparable past make a solid foundation for relationships. This is what we mean when we say we resemble one another. In friendship we look for someone who resonates with the part of us in which we are most our true selves. The part of us that is aware of a strong desire to share experiences with someone who is like us. Eldest daughters recognize each other, as those who attended the Eldest Daughter Day discovered upon coming in the door. Asked how they would describe their best friend, a long list of typical traits followed, including:

- know all about one another
- be able to share and recognize everything
- inspire each other
- shared humour
- wonderfully self-willed
- doesn't judge you
- really understands you
- trustworthy
- is there for you unconditionally
- you can be yourself with
- supports you
- literally feel for each other
- share interests
- laugh together
- chat endlessly
- loyal

In order to find these qualities, many of these women have chosen a friend who is an eldest just like them. With characteristics such as being dutiful, responsible, hands-on, caring and thoughtful, at least you can be sure that the areas of trust, faithfulness and support are covered.

## Uplifting

When you befriend an eldest you can count on her. She will not only feel responsible for her own life but for that of her friends as well, meaning that you can be there for each other in many ways. The Swiss professor, psychotherapist and prolific author Verena Kast wrote a book on friendship between women. Her thesis is that the most reliable friend, with whom there has never been a crisis of confidence, will be seen by a woman as her best friend. She lifts you up. She provides what you need to be able to develop yourself; she is stimulating. She plays an important role in the process of forming and evolving your own personality.

Being too similar also holds a risk, though, cautions Kast; she remarks that the best-friend relationship is susceptible to envy, rivalry and jealousy because you are so close and so alike that you'll want to compare yourselves. Making comparisons can lead in two different directions: you may energize each other with your mutual diligent efficiency, but this quality can also get in the way. Two captains on a ship is one too many. As soon as you get a sense within the friendship that you are competing with one another, it gets complicated. When thoughts start to arise like 'Oh my, she is a better leader, writer, friend or mother than me,' alarm bells should go off. At least if you realize you are going down the slippery slope of starting to believe you are no good at anything.

The fastest way to solve this, Kast says, is to name what is happening to you. Having a best friend means that she is familiar with your shadow side, the parts of yourself you fear most deeply and that you would most fervently like to hide. Daring to share your fears with her is part of what deepens the friendship. The everyday mechanisms of defence are not needed here.

The positive side of the story is that you may also energize each other into excellence. Of course, comparison may lead to heated debates or arguments, but by mirroring each other you also learn to see yourself and your qualities more clearly. When there is no underlying, unspoken or fierce envy, the odds are that all will be well that ends well, even though the disagreements are, of course, not ideal. How fortuitous that, according to the previously mentioned Dr Leman, firstborns more than others within the family are well-versed in making adaptations and changes. In all probability, you as an eldest are quick to spot what is going on in a friendship and what you can do to set things right. This is an area where you can apply what you have learned from a young age.

As two eldest-daughter friends you will no doubt also make fun of all these incredibly familiar, not always charming characteristics that you share – like your meddlesomeness, bossiness and eternal sense of duty. One of the advantages of friendship with kindred spirits is that we fully recognize the urge to work hard and perform as best you can at all times. That we understand how it feels when mistakes are made – even if we are well aware that these make a person learn and grow. That, like all the other firstborns, we think we are the only ones who can solve the issue at hand because we just happen to be the best at it. Ha, ha!

### SHARP AND SEVERE

We don't want to attach the label of being sharp and severe to any eldest daughter (we wouldn't dare), but we are pretty good at it ourselves. While working on this book we kept tabs on the sharp remarks that escaped us at times, and once we started to notice how prickly and strict we could be with each other, we made a point of confronting each other with the things we said – and laughed at ourselves and our firstborn foibles. Below are some samples of ways in which we confronted one another during the weeks we sat together to research this book.

### SEVERE

It is the first day that we're spending together. We're covering the walls of Wies' office with outlines of our research findings and dividing up the tasks of who will dive deeper into which subject. Come time for lunch and Lisette takes the ready-made lentil salad she has brought out of the fridge. 'This is not how we do things in this office,' Wies says. 'We always bring things for each other and there is no quick gobbling up of your food. We take time to sit down and enjoy a meal together.'

### SHARP

Wies loves to wear colourful clothing while Lisette prefers blacks and greys. On the day the photographer comes to take our authors' picture we both happen to wear a burgundy top. 'This is no coincidence, this colour is everywhere these days,' says Wies. 'I have had this jumper for years, fashion colours don't exist,' says the woman who hardly wears any colour at all.

### SEVERE

Conducting research on the Internet, Lisette finds an article on a recent study that concludes that eldest daughters generally achieve very highly. She wants to share this piece of good news on the community Facebook page straight away. Wies: 'Haven't we agreed that we would post things on Wednesdays and Sundays when most people are online?'

### SHARP

While Wies was on holiday, Lisette got completely immersed in researching royal eldest daughters, who thanks to the feminist movement are now eligible to accede to the throne in most countries. This, she argued, restricts them in their freedom of choice, which other women have gained. 'What does that have to do with our topic?' Wies wondered, 'and moreover, who cares?'

### SEVERE

In one of the chapters Wies speaks of the many obstacles that need to be overcome in life. Lisette does not see obstacles but spiritual practice. She doesn't budge. 'Everyone you meet is a master you can learn from. Each time you lose your patience or become angry, you are acting from the personality and not from who you essentially are.' Wies rolls her eyes at this typical strict-eldest-daughter stance. The word 'obstacle' is deleted.

## Befriending a youngest

Although our stocktaking indicated that most eldest daughters opted for another eldest as their best friend, there were also a number of women who had chosen a youngest to occupy this role in their lives. According to Lois Richardson, an eldest sister of sisters will be inclined to befriend women who are youngest and middle children, because she doesn't need to go into competition with them as she would with another eldest daughter. Richardson also points out that eldest daughters with a brother directly below them feel less need for friendship with women. They tend to feel more at home with men, and the other way round – men usually take to them. If they do choose women friends, they do so wishing for this closeness to serve a purpose. The friendship needs to be useful somehow.

While writing this chapter, we asked eldest sisters of one or more brothers on our Facebook page to see if this thesis rang a bell with them. Of the sixty-five women who responded, a little over half were positive. One of them wrote: 'I recognize this. I do have a few good women friends with whom I can speak about matters of the heart but in general I get along better with men. I love the kind of broad-stroke conversations I tend to have with them.' Another response was: 'I have four younger brothers and I used to be real pals with the one right behind me. It is quite probable that as a result of this I never really cared much for girlfriends and to this day I find myself more at ease with men. Realizing what the cause of this is is quite an eye-opener to me.'

Others affirmed their belief that friendship needs to serve a purpose: 'I love what you write about friendship needing to be functional somehow as I have always thought I was a bit strange to set that as a condition. Why couldn't I just natter with friends for hours on end?' And: 'I am the eldest with two younger brothers. I have never been a girls' girl. That is not to say I have not had women friends, but I recognize the need for functionality. I love working with men or at least in mixed gender teams.'

On the other hand, some women with just brothers let us know that they had been bothered by the predominance of testosterone in the family. 'Sports and boys' things were all that mattered. They got the airtime when I was growing up.' These women rejoiced when sisters-in-law made their appearance in the family.

> *'My daughters have always encouraged me to share everything with them and that has been amazing. They are really my best friends, and I think that it is great when you see that transformation from you being the mother and the protector, which in many ways you always remain, to also the relationship changing to being best friends.'*
>
> —— ARIANNA HUFFINGTON on *entrepreneur.com*

An advantage of friendship between an eldest and a youngest daughter is that the different attitude towards life of the youngest – less responsible, freer, easier, looser – may have a liberating influence on you as the eldest. In that sense, a friendship lends itself to finding those qualities in someone else that you yourself would like to possess. In turn, a youngest may find comfort in a friend who takes care of her and gives her good counsel – even if at some point she may feel she has had enough. The risk of the eldest taking on too much of a caring, mothering role is quite real, especially if she has been used to fulfilling such a role at home. Sometimes this pattern has become so strong that she is not aware of it at all. A thirty-year-old photographer, who had never given the fact of being the eldest much thought, all of a sudden understood why she always put a slight distance between herself and her women friends. They all turned out to be youngests. They would call her incessantly, making demands she herself would not make of friends in a million years. She had always taken this division of roles for granted, until this insight into the family pattern repeating itself occurred to her.

Author Deborah Tannen is the middle child of three sisters. She gained worldwide fame with her 1990 book on interpersonal relations *You Just Don't Understand*. Talking with over one hundred women about their sisters, she discovered that in conversation the eldest sister is usually the one who listens, while the younger ones tell stories about their lives. Drawing on their longer life experience, the eldest sisters respond to what is being said and share their insights.

Tannen describes the nature of these conversations as one-sided – friends are generally able to give each other advice and feedback on life experiences without jeopardizing the equality of the relationship, but if one of them continuously occupies the role of advisor, she will appear to be wiser, more experienced and more mature than the other. Just as an elder sister generally is. Tannen emphasizes the depth of the bond between sisters, while also concluding that the hierarchy dictated by the age difference will never fully disappear. This does not need to be the case with friends; the photographer mentioned above discovered a need for a friend who could counsel her for a change, and her options were either to find new friends or to bring the issue up with her existing ones.

## Women friends

The sense of connection and being able to rely on one another is of paramount importance in friendships. Of course, this is not exclusive to eldest daughters. Friendship between women is something to cherish. A friend offers a safe haven in a world that can be fraught with peril. Research confirms that strong friendships exert a positive effect on our health. Sharing your life with other people offers a buffer against stress. The support that you give one another is especially significant, whether that is on the emotional level when you pour your heart out over the break-up of your relationship, or rather more practical when others help you to paint a room or recommend a babysitter you can safely entrust your child to.

Friends are so important to us because generally speaking women understand each other better than men understand women. The mere idea that you can call a friend in an emergency feels supportive. It has even been shown that Dutch women find it harder to picture a life without their women friends than without a partner. Whom to call when divorce looms? What to do when you are exhausted from caring for your aging parents? Or when you tremble now that you have been promoted to the high position everyone else knows you will have no trouble managing? With a friend you can take off your mask. Fears, insecurities, your shadow side – all is welcome here. According to Verena Kast it is incredibly important for women to have a place where they can be themselves. Where they are not afraid that they will be misunderstood or scorned. Where they will not be immediately rebuked, where they can peacefully try to find out what exactly it is that they want.

> *'Naomi Watts and I are very, very good friends and have maintained that through many things... I think that's really rare, particularly for actresses, and I take a lot of pride in that.'*
> — NICOLE KIDMAN in the *Telegraph*

Intense talks with women friends are also hazardous, however. A friend who empathizes too much with the misfortune of another might become 'infected' and you could both end up down in the dumps. You fall into what could be called an empathy spiral. Whether this happens depends on the kind of friend you have. One friend will be more open to emotional infection than another. Identifying fully with the plight of a friend is not always the best way to go; sometimes you are much more use if you can view a situation from a bit of a distance in order to see what exactly is going on.

## Like family

In the early nineteen-eighties Lilian Rubin, the American author, scientist and psychotherapist who died in 2014, attended the wedding of her best friend's son. Upon entering the wedding hall she instantly saw that her friend's family were sitting in the front rows, while friends were placed further behind. The bride's aunt was given a prominent role in the ceremony. Rubin understood

– and yet she felt dismayed. The friendship meant so much to her that she had considered herself to be family – like an aunt – as well, but alas, that was not what she was. Friends are not family. However intimate you are, however deep your conversations go, however strongly your lives are interwoven, one huge difference will always remain: you have not grown up together in the same family; you don't share the same 'language' that was spoken at home, the songs you sang, the jokes that were made; all these memories big and small that are rehashed again and again.

In our Western culture the difference between family and friends is plain to see at crucial life events like weddings and funerals. Rubin's friend could have placed her friend squarely between family members in the front rows. Apparently she thought that was too complicated – or maybe she didn't even give the matter any thought. Many people would no doubt say they see their friends as family, as people who know all about them, to whom they open their hearts. According to Rubin, though, this should first and foremost be seen as a metaphor. The term indicates how much you mean to them. Of course, this metaphor can also be turned round – you can say your sister is your best friend.

In her book *Thrive*, eldest daughter Arianna Huffington more than once describes her younger sister Agapi as her best friend, someone who is always there for her. The familial hierarchy between Arianna and Agapi will, however, never disappear, regardless of how deep their friendship runs.

This difference between friendship and family is, at times, advantageous. As the eldest daughter you may have learned the hard way not to be the one who takes on all the care or organizing. Your friends see you as who you are now. They don't expect you to behave in a typical eldest-daughter fashion. Quite the contrary, when they are aware that you're fed up with that behaviour, they may encourage you to allow yourself greater freedom. Friends can help you not to feel eternally responsible for everyone's well-being. They are the ones to tell you, 'No, my dear, there is no need to call your mother now – let's go see a movie.'

IN BRIEF

- Eldest daughters are often not the easiest ones to befriend.
- Once a friendship is forged, it may well be for life.
- Many eldest daughters have other eldest daughters as their best friend.
- Eldest daughters with a brother right behind them tend to have more friendships with men and are inclined to think friendship needs to have a purpose.
- Friends may feel like family but must take second place when push comes to shove.
- When you and your younger sister are good friends, the hierarchy still remains: the eldest tends to listen and give advice while the younger one shares.

# 8.

# Work with a purpose

• • •

**LISETTE** As a student I read an article in a women's magazine about three young women in Amsterdam. They all ran their own companies. My heart jumps in my chest. This is what I want! Yet my next thought is that this is probably not on the cards for me. I am still set on the narrative that I will marry and have children and do something nice on the side. Not that this image of my future appeals to me, but I have no clue how to escape this pre-programmed life.

Fast-forward eight years and I find myself in a spacious floor on one of Amsterdam's main canals. I have in fact bought the company of one of the women in the article. Wies runs her freelance practice from one of our offices and thus we begin what will prove to be a long life of collaboration. I shape the PR agency for fashion that I bought into an agency for internal corporate communications. With the six of us we write for public magazines, with the emphasis on the corporate world, from the point of view that people are important and will function better when you keep them informed. This was in the days before the Internet, when a computer took up a whole room and no one suspected that we would all carry one in our pockets a few decades later. Directors still dictated letters to their secretaries. People over the age of thirty-five thought they would not have to learn how to handle a computer as this was all a passing fad.

With our short skirts and smart brains we often enter companies at a high level. When ABN Bank wants to begin a video journal, they call us. I don't want to do it. My mind works in words, not in images. However, they are persistent and so every month I present the rough cut in a darkened room to eight men who have to give their consent before the tapes are copied 700 times and distributed in the bank's branches. When Akzo and Nobel merge, we swiftly produce a newsletter in eight languages that employees find on their desks on the day the announcement is made to the press. The large firms in Amsterdam are mystified: for heaven's sake, why do these huge corporations seek out this tiny agency for their prestigious projects? At the time I used to think: because they trust me and us. Because to us they can admit that no one knows how to communicate a computerization program or a merger so well. Because we don't sell them plans but explore with them how to translate the message from the men at the top into words that touch the employees throughout the company in such a way that they don't resist what is happening.

Nowadays I think: because we were eldest daughters. It was not a selection criterion but looking back, I realize that I employed one eldest daughter after another. The success of my company was based on our eldest-daughter skill of conveying our parents' policy to the other children. Translating what those at the top mean – we had been doing this all our lives.

## What do I want?

Even former Euro-commissioner Neelie Kroes, who at a young age displayed a strong will of her own, did what her father thought was best. Touched by the life's work of Albert Schweitzer, she dreamt of studying medicine but in the late nineteen-fifties this subject was not yet taught at the university in Rotterdam where she lived. Her father was fiercely opposed to her taking rooms somewhere else and so she followed his lead, continued to live at home and studied economics. Bursting with ambition, this entrepreneur's daughter embarked enthusiastically on her studies and on student life.

Even women with an academic degree generally, in those days, still became housewives. Young Neelie, however, together with the six other young women in the students' association that she joined, made up a song about their future for a student performance. 'Who knows how important we may become,' they sang, 'for our country's economy, minister or mayor we may be.' In no time this energetic eldest daughter was elected president of her student association. After a career in Dutch politics, she went on to become one of the few women who made it to the top in Europe. Until she stepped down from office in 2014, together with eldest daughters Angela Merkel and Christine Lagarde, she was part of the small circle of visionary women who have made it to the pinnacle of power. She has benefitted from her father's choice. She is not the only one – but not everyone has had such luck.

> *'I can never be safe; I always try and go against the grain. As soon as I accomplish one thing, I just set a higher goal. That's how I've gotten to where I am.'*
>
> — BEYONCÉ KNOWLES on *feelingsuccess.com*

Many eldest daughters are late bloomers. First we follow the beaten track. We do what is expected from us and only when everyone is happy, cared for and able to stand on their own two feet do we get round to ourselves. Then we find space and time for impulses that have lain dormant. Take author Herma van der Weide who recently made her debut. 'A real eldest daughter thing,' she observes, 'to start as an author at age sixty-five.' She hits the nail on the head. Eldest daughters, who from a young age try to keep their parents happy, as a rule need more time to find their own path than others. They are so used to identifying with the values and way of life of their parents that they often are at a loss as to what they themselves want. With their strong sense of responsibility for the welfare of everyone they often forget to wonder what in essence is theirs to do. When they think about a potential profession, others come first. The last thing they want is to be a disappointment to their parents. They feel responsible for setting the stakes high. In a reflection on the Eldest Daughter Day, one of the participants who is in her late sixties wrote, 'It is a vicious circle. Their eyes are upon you, full of expectancy. On this basis you build a strong will to perform well at whatever you do, to meet expectations, without it ever having been discussed openly. It was not a subject of conversation, just feelings and emotions.' She was one among many who had had to make a large detour before realizing that she was valuable in her own right. Not only as eldest daughter or sister, and later as wife or mother, but as the human being that she is.

## Father's will

It is clear that the obedience that eldest daughters display regarding their future, stands in direct relation to the time in which they were born. Parents used to have a bigger say, children were more docile and life seemed more predictable. During the course of our research we met quite a few middle-aged women for whom the detour they had had to make was clearly an issue. At the same time we see that eldest daughters these days still do not feel completely free to disregard their 'parents' – often their father's – wishes.

Fathers in particular usually feel it is their task to make sure their precious one is able to take care of herself. They give this much thought and then, in the way that some men do, they often come up with a highly practical solution. In doing so they are apt to give what is relevant in society more weight than what lives in the girl. They try to predict what skills will be needed and thus come with suggestions for practical studies and subjects with which you will be able to provide for yourself later in life. Often the eldest daughter herself has little insight into forms of education available or their practical application. She has no older sibling to give her an idea of life beyond school. More often than not the advice of her father – especially when she still adores him – weighs heavily when she is making her choice. She may have a sense that she might like to do something else, but once her father has voiced his preference, she can barely remember what it was she herself had imagined. Sometimes she may be somewhat ashamed of her innermost dreams. Or, at least, she is wary of speaking aloud about what she'd like. She cannot even find the right words. Suppose no one understands what she is getting at, or her ideas are found unrealistic and she is scorned? She is not going to risk it; she swallows her own ideas and goes out to do what seems sensible. During the Eldest Daughter Day choices in education and career proved a theme for women old and young. A sixty-year-old eldest daughter had dreamt of becoming a fashion designer, but her father saw no future in an occupation like that; instead she studied medicine and became a doctor. A thirty-year-old eldest studied economics to please her dad but is now trying to get a foothold in fashion.

## Not very original

Can any conclusions be drawn about the kinds of careers that fit eldest daughters best? From the available research, we can see that as eldest daughters we come well-prepared. For longer than children in other birth positions, we are eager to continue our education and we are quite possibly more intelligent in the first place. The effect of our birth position is that from a tender age we have made ourselves into leaders who do what is required with great diligence. Furthermore, from a young age we have been the first ones in our family to do things, and that makes us into habitual pioneers. At the same time we tend to glance over our shoulder to see if our parents approve and if the others are following. We are innovators, working from what already exists. We can improve upon what is given, even greatly improve sometimes. We are good at taking a next step on the basis of what has been done already. But for a fully new idea from left field, for true innovation, you're probably better off with someone else.

In 1871, Charles Darwin found himself speculating about what makes a man the discoverer of undiscovered things, while many others who are very clever – much cleverer than the discoverer – never originate anything. To posthumously honour his great inspirer, Frank Sulloway wanted to answer this question for him. This motivated him enough to read thousands of biographies of people in the fields of politics, science and religion. A bit begrudgingly, as he states in his book *Born to Rebel*, he must acknowledge that family dynamics play a pre-eminent role in human evolution. He never before gave much credence to this line of thinking but when he looks at the data of his research through this lens, it starts to make sense. Relative to their younger siblings, firstborns, according to his findings, are more assertive, socially dominant, ambitious, jealous of their status and defensive. It is natural for them to identify more strongly with power and authority and to employ their superior size and strength to teach the newcomers the house rules. But those younger ones must carve out a place of their own. They serve their own interests by questioning and breaking through the status quo that the firstborn would like to uphold. They rebel. That is why the great historic adventurers and discoverers, iconoclasts and heretics do not come from the legions of the firstborns. People such as Charles Darwin, who brought the world something radically new, generally are not the eldest of the family.

Broadly speaking, Sulloway's conclusion from his historical survey is that the eldest child leans towards leadership and the younger ones towards revolution. The eldest makes people take a next step; later-borns tend to become radicals who push the boundaries. What may also happen is that the eldest plays small in an attempt not to burden the mother, who has her hands full caring for the other kids. This approach may result in a restraint that puts you at a disadvantage when you need to compete for a job.

Given the nature of his research, Sulloway's conclusions are predominantly based on the lives of men, the big figures of history. Researching the lives of firstborn women who have made revolutionary contributions to human history worldwide, we found more than a few firstborn women among them. Amelia Earhart, who was the first woman to fly solo across the Atlantic in 1935, was a daredevil eldest daughter, although she was not the one to invent air travel.

Writer and voice of the second-wave feminist movement Germaine Greer is also a firstborn. She certainly rebelled against the status quo with her view on the predicament of women and spoke sternly against age-old feminine tactics: 'Now as before, women must refuse to be meek and guileful, for truth cannot be served by dissimulation. Women who fancy that they manipulate the world by pussy power and gentle cajolery are fools. It is slavery to have to adopt such tactics.' Her predecessor Simone de Beauvoir, who wrote *The Second Sex*, was an eldest daughter too, who spoke out for women's rights and did not stick to convention in her own life.

Power woman Oprah Winfrey is an eldest, born of a young teenage mother who much later had a second daughter by another man. With her immensely popular television show, there is no question that she has had a huge impact on the lives of many, but is she a true originator? When after twenty-five years and 4,561 episodes she bade farewell to her TV audience she said, 'It is no coincidence that I always wanted to be a teacher. I ended up with the greatest classroom in the world. You all have been a safe harbour for me for twenty-five years. What I hope is that you will be a safe harbour for someone else.'

*'I am regarded as a permanent delayer sometimes, but I think it is essential and extremely important to take people along and really listen to them in political talks.'*

—— ANGELA MERKEL in the *New Yorker*

Our own best guess is that eldest daughters mostly like to do work that matters. They are not the kind to go for a meaningless job just because they like the social environment and then be slackers who sneak off as early as possible at the end of the day. They abhor the idea of watching a movie on the sofa once the children have gone off to school, or of going back to bed. Are you mad? They couldn't do it if they tried. They want to be meaningful to others, make a positive contribution to the organization they are part of, do something useful for society. They don't want to waste their precious time on subjects or projects they don't see the value of. They might make fun of their 'usefulness syndrome' but even so, it has them in a tight grip. Whatever they do, whether it is in healthcare or education or if they are self-employed, it needs to be meaningful. This is a much more important issue for them than the money they make. That someone else benefits from their actions is what keeps them going.

## First fiddle

Eldest daughters learned at our mother's knee to take the lead. Who of us has not been told to take a younger sibling by the hand? Of course, we panicked when the little sister suddenly let go while crossing the street. How do you make such a stubborn kid listen to you so you don't have to panic again the next day? By becoming angry and giving her a good talking-to? Or by quietly putting your hands on her shoulders so she has no way of escaping and you can guide her across safely? It's action learning all the way. Without a guide or a handbook, we develop leadership qualities from a young age. Later in life many of us like playing first fiddle. It's what we have got used to.

Walter Toman is not so appreciative of the way in which eldest daughters lead. His contribution is that he studied the differences between one-gender and mixed families. In his 1961 book *Family Constellation* he describes an eldest sister of sisters likely to be responsible in the workplace, competent, and able to get things done. In a position of leadership she would tend to identify with her boss who must be male in order for her to accept his authority. Females would have to bow to her in order to win her sympathy or mere tolerance, is what his findings at the time showed him. He goes on to say that an eldest sister of sisters would most likely want to be the final authority, work incessantly, give orders to those below her in the company hierarchy and expect them to follow her without protesting.

Over half a century later his lively description seems a bit of a caricature of how we work. We have become much more informal with each other, in many places bosses don't boss others around anymore barking orders, but know they get more done by being supportive and empowering. Yet, if you are an eldest of sisters, you may in your heart of hearts still recognize some of what Toman signalled five decades ago. Even if we don't want to admit to it, somewhere deep inside we may still harbour the little girl who feels like a kind of queen who likes to be attended to.

Still according to Toman, an eldest sister of brothers will display a completely different attitude. In regular working positions, she will not excel but she is fine to have around as she is inclined to create an atmosphere that is conducive to good work being done. In a leading position, he has found eldest sisters of brothers to be generally tactful and inoffensive to people working under her. She is able to delegate work gracefully and expediently. There is just one trait, he signalled, that will lead to antagonism: she tends to be patronizing. When the deadline for a project comes up, she is afraid that too much is asked of her male colleagues while she has much less concern for the women in her team. She is, in a way, protecting 'her little brothers' from overwhelm and overwork. The men in her team might become cagey as a result, while the women in her team sense they aren't valued. Again, these are not very flattering comments from this scientist but for those who dare to look in the mirror, they might hold water. We all tend to project our old family stories onto other people, even more so in stressful situations. A profound look through this lens at the dynamics we engender and keep alive in the workplace, might shed light on what is at the bottom of issues you've never really been able to put your finger on.

> *'I had some female mentors who said, "The media are only going to write about you in one light. So do you want to be a successful businesswoman or do you want to be Mark's silly sister?" I wanted both, but if I had to choose I'd prefer to be taken seriously.'*
>
> — RANDI ZUCKERBERG in the *Daily Telegraph*

The world of work has changed dramatically in the fifty years since Toman's study. This is apparent from Linda Blair's book *Birth Order: What your position in the family really tells you about your character*, published in 2011. Where Toman paints a picture of an orderly work environment where power and rank rule, Blair's starting point is clearly one of collaboration. A psychologist, she grew up in Kansas as the eldest daughter of two medical doctors. She did her psychology studies in the United States and made her career in the United Kingdom, where she worked for the National Health Service, the Medical Research Council and Cambridge University, and had her own weekly radio show.

She warns eldest children not to bite off more than they can chew. They might not agree, she writes, but they will be happiest in a career with someone there to curb their tendency to put pressure on themselves in order to deliver something perfect. She thinks an eldest is probably most satisfied when given the chance to educate others or care for them. Well-established, conventional, proven methods will appeal most: a normal job in healthcare or education, for example. In other words, she reaches a familiar conclusion: we're born to continue, not to renew.

This seems to correspond with the occupations of the women from our study. Eleven of the sixty-one who filled in their occupation work in healthcare. Seven called themselves managers, others facilitators, trainers, researchers and consultants. Seven worked in education; there was a judge, an interior designer and a real estate agent. Two women indicated they were housewives and no fewer than nineteen said they were self-employed as copywriters, a make-up artist and a woman who described herself as a 'pearl diver'. We think she works as a life coach and probably she was not the only one present. In no way do we want to contend that this is a statistically representative group, yet they do seem representative of the types of occupations that eldest daughters flourish in.

## Afraid to be bossy

Eldest daughters who are born leaders do not always understand why they are one of the few who climb to the top. One such woman is Sheryl Sandberg, chief operating officer of Facebook, where one in five world citizens share their life events on a daily basis. When she got married, to a man who sadly died suddenly in May 2015, her younger brother and sister took the mickey out of her. They made a big play out of how they had always had to walk a few steps behind Sheryl while she carried on long monologues. The wedding guests were amused, of course. So was the bride – but at the same time she caught herself in a judgement she had not expected to make: that it is not right for a girl to be so dominant. This thought momentarily took her aback. Would even she, a woman who so actively wants to stimulate other women to 'lean in', when push comes to shove be of the opinion that a woman should not be proactive in taking the lead? She calls herself old-fashioned but apparently the belief that as a woman you have to hold back a bit is deeply rooted, she concludes in her 2013 book *Lean In*.

Another reason why women are wary of stepping up to the plate is the fear of not being liked; they are freaked out by the idea that they could be seen as 'bossy'. Here Sandberg hits a sore point. That fear of being seen as bossy is one we saw in our study time and again. Which eldest daughter does not have a picture of the family's children on the sofa together with cuddly animal toys, while she sits or stands in front of them playing the teacher? 'My father once filmed how I played with the others,' Stephanie said. She is almost thirty and the eldest of four. 'No, you are that, I told my sister. You can see that she was not happy with the role I gave her, but still she did as I said. She was pleased to be allowed to play in the first place.'

And then there is the inner voice that reminds many women of what might go wrong. 'Are you sure you are right?' the critic asks when you make a statement. 'Do you really think you can do that?' whispers something inside you when you take on a new task. If you lend an ear to these doubts, then making a career is going to be hard; of course, it would be easier to stay on the sidelines.

Being bossy is not something to strive for. For whatever reasons, this term is only used about women. 'He is such a bossy man,' is not something you ever hear. Yet everyone has heard of bossy women. And, often, they involuntarily shudder. This is not the kind of woman you'd prefer to be around, so you would not want to be one either.

The Netherlands is known as a country that favours traditionally feminine values such as modesty, service and solidarity. But from reading Sheryl Sandberg, being bossy doesn't seem to be a good thing for a woman in the United States either with its generally more masculine culture.

## Leadership and ego stuff

Christine Lagarde, the French former lawyer, manager and minister who since 2011 has been the first woman to head the International Monetary Fund, gives striking descriptions of leadership. Her father passed away when she was sixteen. As the eldest of the family, she had to support her mother and help her younger brothers. So she learned early in life that terrible sorrow and grief never really go away, while at the same time she felt empowered to make something of her life and help others do the same. She has a theory that women are generally given space and appointed to jobs when the situation is tough. 'In times of crisis, women eventually are called upon to sort out the mess, face the difficult issues and be completely focused on restoring the situation,' she says. It is as if she is describing situations in which it is OK to be bossy for a while – or maybe she has found ways to get a lot done without seeming to be bossy.

Hardly anyone functions at her level but if you lead any kind of team, department or company, your style of leadership might resemble hers: 'To me, leadership is about encouraging people. It's about stimulating them. It's about enabling them to achieve what they can achieve – and to do that with a purpose. Others would call it "a vision", but I'd rather use "purpose" because I think that everybody has a purpose in life, and that when collectively people work together, or practise sport together, they have a joint purpose.'

Another thing this woman at the top does is to see things in perspective: 'When I sit in meetings and things are very tense and people take things ex-tremely seriously and they invest a lot of their ego, I sometimes think to myself, "Come on, you know, there's life and there's death and there is love." And all of that ego business is nonsense compared to that.'

In the Netherlands, Melanie Schultz van Haegen, who in her mid-forties is already a consummate government official who now serves as cabinet minister of Infrastructure and Environment, is also happy to discuss this subject. In our interview with her she said that she had never before given any thought to the influence of place in the family, but now that she herself is mother to an eldest daughter she recognizes patterns from her own youth. 'When the children fight, as parents you tend to request from her that she please behave. You ask this of her when she is six and her brother a toddler, but when he is six, you still ask her. If he goes to a sports club that she has already joined, you ask her if she can please take him along. I have no doubt that it leaves an impact to be required to take responsibility as the eldest in this way, but I am not sure there is any difference between eldest boys or girls.'

A trait she recognizes in her own eldest daughter is a certain awe of authority, a wanting to do things the way they are supposed to be done. 'I have lost this mainly thanks to my husband,' she says. 'We met when I was quite young, still in high school. He is a second child and he showed me I could go off the beaten track. "Why behave like people expect?" he would ask. Ever since then I have consciously explored the boundaries of my comfort zone. I see mistakes as opportunities to learn. When I first left politics and started working with a big insurance firm, I had to learn to operate within a more collegiate culture. I was much too authoritative. When, in the first meeting I chaired, I described how I would like to work, the others looked at me askance. In the political arena one steers from content; in a company, process and human capital are equally important. From this experience in the corporate world I have expanded my repertory of leadership styles and now I can adapt according to the role I'm in.'

## Being worth it

When you want to go far in the world, you have to be able to put things into perspective. And you have to be thick-skinned. High-flyers like Hillary Clinton, Angela Merkel and Melanie Schultz van Haegen are often the target of criticism. They have to be able to deal with people who completely disagree with them, who write harsh comments in newspapers and express undiluted criticism of the policies they propose. They will no doubt have moments when this hits home; they may even shed a tear at times – but they stand their ground.

Melanie Schultz van Haegen: 'I do observe a kind of apathy in young eldest daughters that I know when things don't go as they had planned. When someone criticizes them or comes up with an alternative plan, they can just run off and not want to play at all any more. I can't remember doing that myself. I have a kind of basic inner security that usually makes me appreciate people telling me how things can be done in other ways than mine. I do also recognize being a pioneer. Every time I took a step into the unknown, I have always felt secure in the knowledge that I would find my feet.'

113

Others might have more of a struggle with the inner voice that whispers and says that underneath your competent image you are in fact a cheat who doesn't amount to much. Even Sheryl Sandberg is prone to this phenomenon. She discovered that there is even a term for this recurring doubt of one's own capacities: impostor syndrome – the perpetual fear of being found out as not being good enough. It is her impression that women tend to underestimate themselves. When given a compliment, you only think of everything you don't know and you don't even hear what the person tells you. Even when you do know your business, you still think that it should have been done differently or better. Sometimes you can learn from those who came after you in the family. Sandberg observes the natural self-confidence of the brother who is two years her junior. 'At times when I lack confidence, I pretend,' she says. 'The miracle is that when I do, I immediately feel more sure of myself.'

From an early age we are used to stepping into the unknown without any prior knowledge, be it going to kindergarten, to school, college or entering the job market. Time and again we start out on a new adventure without having someone we can copy. Some dub our unsuspecting attitude naive, but the life lessons that we have learned on the way may also boost our self-confidence. We leave our youth with a treasure trove of capabilities. We can do things and need not be bossed around by anybody.

This is affirmed by Christine Lagarde who, despite her high-level position, still has men patronizing her. She falls back on the mantra repeated to her by her synchronized-swimming coach when she was young: 'When it's tough, grit your teeth and smile'. So that is what she does: 'The best defence when that happens is a solid sense of humour,' she says. 'At the end of the day, these men are human beings as well. They have wives, they have daughters.' Only to add, 'In the face of adversity, go. They don't deserve you.' Of course, not many of us function at the top levels of the eldest daughters cited above. We don't need to. You make a difference wherever you are. That is where you matter. That is where it is important that you know your own value and that you don't go out of your way to make others happy. If you are courageous enough to believe in yourself, for women with capacities such as ours there is a whole world to be won. A lovely compliment in this respect was paid to eldest daughter Whoopi Goldberg, when for family reasons she had been absent from her job as co-host of *The View*, the Emmy Award-winning American daytime talk show. 'We missed you,' her colleagues said when she joined them again, 'You are truly the captain of this ship.'

## IN BRIEF

- Many eldest daughters are late bloomers, often because they have initially taken up a career path that their father thought sensible.
- Without manuals, as little girls we develop leadership capacities based on life experiences.
- Many firstborns suffer from 'impostor syndrome' – believing that at any given moment they may be found out as 'not good enough'.
- For eldest children, usually the most appealing work is that in which you are of immediate importance to others.
- You're bound to be happiest in a career in which you can curb your tendency towards perfectionism and alleviate some of the pressure you put on yourself.
- Eldest daughters have no qualms taking a step into the unknown; they have been used to doing that all along.
- Eldest daughters are innovators; however continuity is their foremost concern.

# 9.

# True love

...

**LISETTE** His voice still thick with sleep, my partner Jos said one day: 'I dreamt you were going away for six months to do something with whales. Then I'll be out of here, is what I said.' He knows this is my greatest fear: that I do what is mine to do in the world and that one day he will be fed up. Fed up with me being away so many evenings, taking trips to do a workshop, attend a conference or have meetings. Sometimes, when he is off to the pub round the corner, the fear creeps up on me. 'What if he doesn't come back because I am such a handful?' an anxious inner voice whispers inside me. This is my old fear of being too much, being too self-willed in leading my own life, not being suited to live with someone else.

Just like my sister who is four years my junior, Wies found the love of her life at high school. I needed much longer than them. I had several boyfriends while at university but I could never completely be myself with them. When it was over, it always felt as if I could spread my wings again. Having settled in Amsterdam, I was not successful in love at all. Men seemed to like me well enough as an entrepreneurial type, but usually it did not take me long to find out that they assumed that I would soon start to iron their shirts.

Jos is fully independent. In truth, he doesn't really need me for any-thing, as is the case for me. At the same time, we need each other badly for the sense of humour that we share, our perspective on life, the narrative of our lives that we follow closely, the way we hold the mirror up for one another and the natural warmth between us as we each sit on our own sofa reading a book at the weekend.

In 1998, when I first came to Findhorn, the spiritual centre in the north of Scotland where I now serve as the chair of the trustees, I wanted to move there. I yearned to immerse myself in the exquisite way in which people there live in harmony with each other, with nature and the will of the divine. I called Jos and told him. The answer of this youngest son, with whom I had been in a relationship for four years at the time, still dazzles me: 'You've got to do what you've got to do.' I did not move to Findhorn as I did not want to leave him and life in that community is not his thing. He is an abstract painter and I am involved in initiatives at the edge of consciousness and societal renewal. Thus we both lead our own lives, much as I did when I was young. For hours I would sit in my room engrossed in my own world as if living on an island, while my brother and sister were out with friends, doing sports or participating in other social engagements. This is what Jos has been used to, too; he spends his days in the silence of his own studio. Growing up with three elder sisters taught him how to deal with women. You have to let them be and not respond to their every whim. This is how he is with me. When I come home excited about a topic that seems to me utterly fascinating, he listens with equanimity. He'll wait and see if it proves to be an enduring passion or just a fleeting interest. When I scrutinize books on yet another method of conscious living, he quietly asks if the other stack of books can be put in storage. When I bite off more than I can chew and am on a short fuse with him, with just a look he lets me know this is not how we agreed to be with one another. I praise my good fortune that he gives me these early warning signs so we don't come to the point of no return that I so fear. He just shakes his head at my fears, saying there is no need, as long as I don't disappear on him to rescue the whales.

## Huge happiness

Waking up together in the morning and having a lie-in. Having friends over for dinner in the evening and reflecting on the conversations while clearing up afterwards. That the other then makes a comment that offers you a new perspective. Or just the two of you, watching a series on Netflix. Being relaxed together and not having to pretend in any way. Cracking jokes that no one else would understand or like but that for you affirm your relationship. Not every day is idyllic in the business of a life that has a lot going on, but finding a person who wants to share your life is a huge happiness.

We asked about this aspect of life during the Eldest Daughter Day. Is your partner an only child, an eldest, a middle child or a youngest? Of the sixty-one women who participated in this review, three indicated their partner was an only child, fifteen share their lives with an eldest, twenty-one with a middle child and twenty-two with a youngest. They were happy to disclose what brought them happiness in their relationship: 'We are good friends. We stimulate each other to develop further. We theorize, talk and laugh together. We listen to one another and complement each other.' And also: 'We are each other's opposites. He has a much more relaxed attitude and he keeps me grounded in reality. He respects me. He wants to support me in what I do and is always on my side. He wants only the best for me. He is there for me unconditionally.'

## The same and different

From time immemorial the great game of love has had two basic rules, which anyone who gives it a moment's thought will be able to produce straight away:

- Birds of a feather flock together '
- Opposites attract

At first glance these two sayings seem contradictory. They are not. You need enough resemblance to be able to recognize yourself in each other and you need to differ enough to be able to remain fascinated by each other.

For continuity's sake it is helpful in a relationship that you are more or less interested in the same kinds of things, share the same values and sense of humour. You are not the same and never will be, but alikeness is helpful in being able to identify with your partner in life. This is a prerequisite for being able to understand and have a sense of each other, however different you appear to be. In the busy lives we lead these days it is also just practical when you want to spend your free time in much the same way. Should children appear on the scene, it also helps greatly if your notions on how to raise them do not diverge too widely.

At the same time, in order to keep a relationship interesting, variety is essential. As long as you are able to keep surprising your partner with your perspective or insight, you may continue to captivate each other for years. The occasional difference of opinion with your significant other only contributes to staying open, to seeing things differently than just from your particular point of view. Going places where you would have never gone by yourself enriches your life. The measure in which you are different provides the exchange that keeps both of you learning and growing. As long as the gap does not become too wide to bridge, the mutual dissimilarities keep the relationship lively.

## The duplication theorem

Walter Toman can take credit for the discovery of the third ground rule. Based on the research he conducted in his years at Brandeis University in Massachusetts, his recommendation is: duplicate the situation in your family. From his research into the impact of birth order the psychologist concluded that the role a person has had in early intra-familial relationships will carry over into adult relationships. According to him, people will subconsciously tend to fall in love with and ultimately bind themselves to someone with whom they feel at ease because of the similarities with what they were used to while growing up. His data showed him that relationships in which you are complementary relative to your birth position give the best chance of longstanding happiness. In other words: a heterosexual eldest daughter is best matched with a youngest son who grew up with one or more older sisters. A youngest son with older brothers may also do, but according to Toman, a man with sisters is the number one favourite.

This is not a very sexy piece of advice. Quite the contrary. How adventurous can it be to replicate the situation at home when you are eager to spread your wings and make a life for yourself? This, of course, is not what you've been waiting to hear. Yet, there it is. We grow up not on our own as unconnected islands but through innumerable interactions on a daily basis with those around us. You play together passionately until all of a sudden you get into a fight and never want to lay eyes on each other again. A little while later you find yourself watching a movie together, sharing a snack. You learn how to make amends after having exploded. You are on to each other's weak and tender spots, you can drive each other up the wall. You know each other like the back of your own hand, you learn to live together and how to make things light and pleasant for everyone. In the meantime you form each other more than you may realize. Later in life you will continue to do all kinds of things in the ways that you were used to at home, that you learned and developed together with your siblings and that feel familiar and comfortable to you. The role you played while growing up will be the one you'll find yourself fulfilling over and over again later in life.

> 'Wholehearted people fully embrace vulnerability as they believe that what makes them vulnerable makes them beautiful. They have the willingness to say "I love you" first, to do something without guarantees, to invest in a relationship that may or may not work out.'
>
> —— BRENÉ BROWN in her 2010 TEDx Houston Talk

Toman's findings stem from the middle of the twentieth century when we still pretended homosexual relationships simply did not exist. When, worse still, in some nations they were banned by law. As far as we have been able to gauge, no research has yet been done into the influence of birth order on happiness in gay relationships. What we have found are allusions to the fact that partnerships between women sometimes cave in under the excessive drive from both partners to take care of each other. Although we name the quality of caring as one of the main characteristics of eldest daughters, we can, however, not turn the tables and maintain that this excessive caring is exclusive to relationships between eldest daughters. Nor can we state that a homosexual eldest daughter will find her best match in a youngest sister of sisters. This doesn't mean we are not curious about whether this would indeed be the case.

## The perfect youngest son

In his 2009 book *Strangers in a Strange Lab* William Ickes, distinguished professor in the department of psychology at the University of Texas at Arlington, goes as far as to say that men who grew up with an older sister should give her a call and thank her profusely. Why? Because the odds are that if they have had some success with women in their lives, this is due to what they learned from observing – and having to deal with – her. Ickes has studied Toman's work deeply and wanted to test the predictions from his family constellation theory.

Studies on how women with a brother and men with a sister communicate generally show that people who come from mixed-gender families understand the other sex better than people from families consisting of girls or boys only. This seems to make sense, but Ickes added a salient aspect to his research that has implications for eldest daughters – he wanted to find out if he could spot a marked difference between people with an older sister or brother and those with one or more younger siblings. He could. When put in dyads, the men who grew up with older sisters hit it off markedly better with their female partners than the men who grew up with younger sisters. They also asked their female partners many more questions. In turn, they got a very favourable reception from the women, who rated them as being significantly more self-assertive, exciting and friendly. The women in the study looked at these men longer than they had at those with younger sisters – a long look rather than a quick glance indicates liking – which makes sense: who doesn't like a man you can conduct a real conversation with?

In *The Birth Order Book of Love*, published in 2008, William Cane goes even further. He came across an article by Walter Toman as a student and from then on made it a point to find out the birth order of all his friends at college. Though there were exceptions, he found that most fitted the pattern. When he started to teach English, he asked his students and continued his observations. Travelling across North America after the success of his first book, on the art of kissing, he asked the couples he invited up front to demonstrate. This gave him a front-row seat to observe how diligent two firstborns tend to be with each other, how chaotic two last-borns were, how last-born girls love the chance to be seen in front of an audience and how last-born guys love to get the laughs. A firstborn himself, he took to teaching like a duck to water. He doesn't teach English any more, but he lectures about birth order and its impact on your relationships at college. The students love his sessions. Finally someone who shines a light on the murky field of love.

'The darling of the gods' is how Cane describes the younger brother of sisters. 'They think of you no matter where you are or what you do,' he writes, 'they dream of you, and they want to be yours. And you, doing nothing to draw them in but being your own sweet self, you're blessed above all men when it comes to attracting the fair sex.' After thirty-eight years of surveying, he gives a number of reasons that sound very plausible:

- Since the older sister was usually the serious one, the youngest son may have honed his comic genius, his creative streak.
- To make his parents notice him and to get his sister to stop teasing him, he developed into a friendly, agreeable and socially conscious young man.
- Being the youngest, he cares for the underdog and under-reported issues, whether it's minorities treated badly or animal species under threat of extinction (like Marlon Brando, a younger brother of sisters, declining the Academy Award on the basis that the American film industry had treated Native Americans poorly).
- He has more intuitive insight into how people feel than other boys.

- A youngest brother of sisters has a knack for getting along with girls and making them like him.

There may, however, be a downside to all of this. As eldest sisters our younger brothers may have put us on a pedestal and adored us to the point that no one else comes close. A youngest son can be irked no end by his eldest sister, especially when she wants to mother him too much to be palatable to him, while at the same time admiring her. She is out there doing what she does. His future partner will have to measure up to her. So yes, a younger son with sisters is generally the best match for an eldest daughter, but only after having let go of his adoration for his own eldest sister.

## Clashing firstborns

One quarter of the women who attended the Eldest Daughter Day indicated that their partner was an eldest, too. Researchers in this field would raise their eyebrows. We don't want to stir up strife in good partnerships, but data has it that two eldests together are not always the easiest of combinations. Two first-borns sharing their lives may lead to what has been called 'conflict on the basis of rank'. A family has a hierarchy. However different children of one family may be, whatever the successes are that they achieve once they have left home and found their way in the world, the hierarchical birth position is implanted deep within. An eldest (please forgive a little exaggeration) is used to taking the lead when it comes to taking important decisions, seeing what needs to be done and dividing the tasks. Below are Frank Sulloway's characteristics of firstborns. An ardent admirer of Charles Darwin, his point of departure is ceaseless sibling competition for the undivided attention of the parents. It is a good idea when looking at his list of qualities to bear in mind that his research is predominantly based on powerful historic figures, i.e. men. From raking through thousands of biographies he finds these to be the most common qualities of eldest sons:

- dominant
- firm

- competitive
- not very flexible
- not very emphatic
- conservative
- conventional
- easily irked

Compare these with the big five qualities that we have found typical of eldest daughters – responsible, thoughtful, dutiful, hands-on and caring – and you can see it coming. Two firstborns together will not always have an easy time. As long as the love flourishes, all might be hunky-dory, but as soon as the first flush of love is over, issues big and small will be discussed by two people who are both used to things going their way.

Cane compares firstborns with heads of state. Both feel presidential, so why should either one defer to the other? Perhaps they might decide to work together on a mutually beneficial project, he writes, but even if they do, who is to set the direction and organize the proper approach? You can be sure, he concludes, that no matter what they do or how they arrange their time together, two firstborns will always feel the effects of rank conflict because they're both leaders.

## Royal choices

There is an extraordinary category of eldests who seem to do very well with other eldests. Almost without exception in the past decade, European crown princes have married firstborn women. This may hark back to a time-honoured tradition in which the eldest daughter was the main prize when it came to strategic alliances between royal and noble families. It would have been unacceptable to fob off the English or French king with a youngest, even if she would have suited him better in temperament or character than her solid eldest sister. Still, the firstborn was the prize pawn for both crown and throne.

Nowadays princes don't need to marry another royal. They are free to make their own choice. Yet a remarkable number of them have still opted for eldest daughters. Europe's oldest crown prince, Charles, Prince of Wales, heir apparent to the thrones of the Commonwealth, did not make a good match with Diana, who was a middle child with two elder sisters and a younger brother. He has long been in love with Camilla Parker-Bowles, who is an eldest just like him. His eldest son William married Kate Middleton, now Catherine, Duchess of Cambridge, who is an eldest of three. In interviews in the press she has mentioned how nervous she was at the beginning about all the protocols that came with her new role as wife of the second in line to the throne. When asked how she deals with that, she confirms that she is willing to work hard to master court manners, thereby proving herself to be a true eldest daughter.

The Belgian King Philippe, too, married an eldest, a member of the untitled nobility Mathilde d'Udekem d'Acoz, making her the first Belgian-born queen consort of the country. His namesake Felipe of Spain married former journalist and news anchor Letizia Ortiz, an eldest of three sisters whom he met at a dinner party. One day this divorcee was presenting the evening news and the next day, with the official announcement of her engagement to the Prince of Asturias who has since ascended to the throne, she was the news herself.

> 'Dave was my rock. When I got upset, he stayed calm. When I was worried, he said it would be OK. When I wasn't sure what to do, he figured it out. I am grateful for every minute we had.'
> — SHERYL SANDBERG on *Facebook*

In the Netherlands, Argentinian-born Máxima Zorreguieta Cerruti, the wife of King Willem-Alexander, is the first Dutch queen consort since 1890. In 2013, the man she married in 2002 succeeded his mother Beatrix, a typically responsible, dutiful and studious eldest of four sisters, to the throne. With two younger sisters and one younger brother, Queen Máxima is the eldest daughter of her mother while also having three half-sisters from an earlier marriage of her father's. When Willem-Alexander announced his succession to the throne on national television, he told the story of how their eldest daughter Amalia hadn't missed a beat in asking him how long he was planning to hold this job. She is obviously well aware of what awaits her.

## Middle options

How about eldest daughters with a partner who is a middle-born? Middle children are not so easily described; they come in all forms and shapes. The eldest knows her position as it never changes, even after others are born. Only one can be the eldest, but middle children, who have each been the youngest for a while, have no such certainty. They are the youngest only until a next one comes along, at which point everyone moves up a step on the family ladder. If there is a somewhat longer pause between births, little groupings can appear within the family. In the big families of old there used to be a definite order in the middle range. Thus you'd have middle children who described themselves as the youngest of the older bunch or the eldest of the young ones.

Within the smaller families that have become the norm in many places nowadays, the middle-borns form the bridge, on their own or sometimes two of them. Looking up they see what they have yet to learn; looking down they see what they have already mastered. With the bulk of parental attention focusing on the eldest and the youngest, many are not sure how to define their role within the family. So, often they choose to try their luck outside the home. To avoid being dependent on their parents' appreciation, they forge close friendships with others outside of the family sphere. This chosen family may become more important to them than their blood family. With their adaptive personalities and openness to new experiences, they are often popular and able to maintain a circle of friends drawn from many walks of life.

In their book *The Secret Power of Middle Children*, published in 2011, psychologist Catherine Salmon and journalist Katrin Schumann want to shepherd the multifaceted and, in their view, often underestimated middle-borns into the limelight. Their ten years of research points to three essential characteristics of middle children's personalities:

- dedication to chosen family
- agreeableness
- openness to experience

Middles don't like conflict, the authors say, and they will often be the first to try to make amends. They are, however, not averse to a good fight and see a heated exchange of arguments not so much as a battle but rather as a way to gain useful information on all sides of an issue. As the frequent middleman in disputes among siblings, they've taught themselves to be agreeable, to defuse disagreeable situations, avoid extremes and focus on getting the deal done in whatever way seems most effective. Generous with their time and their attention, they are highly social beings. Unfailingly giving and dedicated, they are more likely to give valuable presents to friends than either first or last-borns. Solid and flexible, they are altruistic team players. Being great listeners, they need to remember to stand up for themselves at times instead of being self-effacing in keeping the many members of their chosen family of friends happy and content. They may display a tendency to avoid confrontation and, with their excellent emotional intelligence, go the way of the peaceful warrior who is more successful with words than with swords. With all these qualities, according to the authors, loyal, kind and clever middle children make excellent partners both for firstborns – whom they describe as 'dominant and assertive' – and also for last-borns, who in their eyes 'like only children, tend to be more spoiled and stubborn'.

## What about you?

There is another side to this story. What kind of a partner does an eldest daughter make? A good one, no two ways about it, of course. When we find a mate who takes us as we are, we can relax and beautifully live the qualities that characterize us. There may be some work involved, however, before we get to that point. Just as youngest sons might have to take their eldest sister down from the pedestal they have put her on, many a firstborn woman has to release something before they can find true love. This act of releasing concerns, of course, the father, whom eldest daughters are inclined to revere more than their siblings. He was the first man in their lives, sometimes their support and comfort when the next children came along. She looked to him for approval and he might have looked back at her with a special gleam in his eye, for she was his first one, too. Thus, at least in the perception of the young girl, they had a special, exclusive bond. The title of Gwyneth Paltrow's first recipe book says it all: *My Father's Daughter*. She calls her dad Bruce the first love of her life, and as he loved to cook for those he held dear, she loved to help him. The beautifully illustrated book contains not only many of his recipes but also a picture of his favourite kitchen knife, which after his death in 2002 became hers.

As long as in your heart of hearts you hold your father to be the ideal man, there surely is no real space for someone else; you have to clear that space first. Sometimes this just happens of its own accord; sometimes you need the help of friends to point out to you in a subtle way that you seem to hold your father as infallible, when in fact he is just a man, with good and weaker sides like everybody else.

> *'My husband is here and I'd like to thank him, for many things, but first of all for pointing out that I had a big hole in my frock and then that my nipples were pointing in different directions. It's good to have an expert there to help you with that sort of thing.'*
>
> —— EMMA THOMPSON at the *Empire Film Awards*

Family constellations are a trans-generational therapeutic intervention that has its roots in family systems therapy. Within this body of work it has often been observed how the eldest daughter takes the place of her mother next to her father. In one of his first books on the subject, *Love's Hidden Symmetry*, psychotherapist Bert Hellinger makes the observation that 'people entering into relationships with the hope – acknowledged or not – that they get something they didn't get in their relationships with their mothers or fathers, are looking for parents. The belonging that then develops is that of child and parent. When a woman is still tied to her father, she often secretly believes that she would be a better partner for him than her mother is. That's a child's belief. If a woman remains a daughter looking for a father, the relationship is not the relationship of an adult woman and man.' Outer circumstances such as a prolonged illness or early death of the mother may have been the cause of the eldest daughter taking up the place next to the father. When the eldest starts to mother the other siblings, it often causes confusion and irritation. The eldest herself can subsequently experience difficulty finding a partner as this position in her life is already taken.

The family constellation method works with statements spoken, between participants in the group, to restore the right order within the 'family' represented by the group and thus liberate everyone involved. In this case the person representing the eldest may say to her 'parents': 'You are my mother, I am your daughter and that is my role' and 'You are my father, I am your daughter, I am not your partner' and the representatives of the parents may affirm this in turn. When these things are spoken out loud, even though the participants are not real family members and may be strangers, the balance is restored and healing happens not only to the one who was present but, more often than not, inexplicably to the whole family system.

Another predicament may be that you want to try and be 'wonderwoman', the ideal partner, lover, mother and spouse. It may have become clear by this point that such an endeavour is doomed to fail. Moreover, if you are not willing to be seen as you are in your most intimate relationship, when will you allow yourself to be known? Firstborn Brené Brown gives good advice on this matter. She realized that in order to feel a true sense of belonging, she needed to bring her real self out and that the only way to achieve this was through practising self-love. She had always thought it was the other way around: that she would feel accepted by doing whatever it took to fit in, and that as a result she would feel better. Only once she realized how much effort she was making, did she understand why she had felt exhausted for so long.

A partner who sees all of us, who protects us from being overly zealous and caring, who makes us realize that life is not about what we do and can do, however important in the outer world, but about who we truly are – we wouldn't begrudge anyone such a partner. As dynamic firstborns we need a safe haven where we can kick off our shoes, cuddle up close to someone and not have to be the oldest and the wisest for a change.

## IN BRIEF

- For lasting happiness: duplicate the situation in your family.
- According to that rule an eldest daughter is best paired with a youngest son who has elder sisters.
- Youngest sons with elder sisters come with experience of what women think and expect.
- Sometimes, finding love requires an eldest daughter to let go of the idea that her father is the perfect man.
- Allowing for exceptions, an eldest daughter will have the most conflicts with a partner who is an eldest, too.
- Most European crown princes in recent years have married eldest daughters.

# 10.

# An eldest daughter of your own

. . .

**WIES**  Pregnant with my first child, I received all kinds of well-meant advice. It got to be so much that I even wrote a column about it. I cannot recall my exact words but I do remember the gist of my argument: I was exasperated. I felt everyone was expressing opinions on what would surely be a most natural and spontaneous process: becoming a mother. I found it curious and sometimes even scary that strangers would put their hands on my tummy to feel whether I was going to have a boy or a girl. I got annoyed with books telling me all manner of things that, carrying a child, I should or should not do. A friend described to me how, while pregnant, a woman had slapped a cigarette out of her hands when she was visibly enjoying her smoke. Of course, smoking during pregnancy is not the thing to do – but to slap a cigarette from someone's fingers? I was outraged about such an invasive act – and I had my column in which to vent my anger. Typing away, I poured out my annoyance about how all and sundry felt a right to meddle in pregnant women's affairs. What do you mean, getting the baby's room ready three months in advance?

With the self-confident superiority of a first-timer I ignored all advice with disdain, including that from people saying we were crazy to move house a few days before the baby was due. We had arranged it so that I did not have to carry a thing. It all looked highly doable, except for the fact that our new house was not quite finished. The bathroom had some essential features missing, there was no lighting in the bedroom nor did we have any curtains yet. It all looked fine to me. In a few days' time we had unpacked a lot of our boxes. Then Didi was born. In a bedroom lit only by a flashlight and with a midwife who first refused to come – thinking my husband Wim and I were grossly exaggerating the pace of my contractions – which resulted in us staying home as we would never have been able to get to the hospital where I had planned to give birth in time.

The moment Didi arrived, everything changed. The euphoria about our first one lasted for weeks on end. What a miracle child! We were convinced that she could in no way be compared to any of the other babies we had laid eyes on in our lives. Life without her immediately seemed inconceivable. In the wave of emotions we both tried our best to come up for air from time to time. Our whole life was completely and utterly gobbled up by a sleeping, crying and eating 3.3-kilogram dolly. When Didi regurgitated half the milk she had been drinking so sweetly, stricken with panic we leafed through the books I had recently rebuffed so haughtily. 'Projectile vomiting,' my sister read out loud. She, too, was settling into her new role as proud aunt. What a disaster. We called the midwife, who again refused to come. This time, fortunately, she was right.

As laid-back as I had been during the pregnancy about all the advice I was given, the more eager for information I became after our daughter's birth. I had become a mother. On the one hand this felt completely natural and good; on the other hand I hit a brick wall on issues I had not been able to envisage beforehand. Innumerable children are being born and raised each and every day. I trusted my intuition, and Wim, of course. I was partially right to do so. Yet I was delighted to have within easy reach the books that I had previously given the cold shoulder. Going to the child welfare clinic armed with friends' advice helped me not be intimidated by the stern talks based on the holy norm of the average growth chart. I realized that I could make countless mistakes, because there was so much I didn't know. I had become a mother for the first time – a life event like no other.

## A mother's love

She, your firstborn, turned your life upside down. Everything completely changed with her arrival in a way that no one could have spelled out to you beforehand. You will never forget the moment she saw the light of day. Whatever her age now, she remains the one who turned you into a mother. She was the first to make you aware of the vast quantity of motherly love you possess. Even if later children have evoked those same tender feelings in you again, it was with her that you experienced this overwhelming love for the first time and that will always remain special. However many books on pregnancy and childbirth you might have read, however many stories experienced mothers might have told you, there is no way of knowing before it happens.

As a gynaecologist, author Dr Christiane Northrup assisted innumerable mothers with giving birth before she herself became a mother. Even she describes her own first time as altogether overwhelming. Apparently, as with many other life events, going through this yourself is crucial. It happens instantly: you deem your baby to be the greatest miracle the world ever saw. As soon as this baby is born, you know for a fact that you will do whatever it takes to love and protect her. Unconditionally you throw yourself into the endeavour of making your child happy.

All of a sudden you and your partner are not a couple anymore, but a family. A family that keeps growing. With the arrival of number two, your firstborn becomes an eldest just like you. What does this mean for her? Will she fulfil this role in the same way that you used to? Or will things pan out differently, because she has a mother who is an eldest herself? Also, what does it mean for you to have a daughter who in this one aspect at least resembles you a lot? Do you recognize yourself in her? Do you intend to do things in not the same way at all as your own mother did? Or will history repeat itself?

## Your own mother

No childhood experience is as intense as the relationship of a young girl with her mother, says Christiane Northrup in her book *Mother–Daughter Wisdom*. At a cellular level we all carry within us an imprint of how our mother felt as a woman, how she looks at her own body, how she takes care of herself and what she thinks is possible in life; what is her view. Our mother's beliefs and her behaviour set the tone for how we will take care of ourselves as adults. While it is true that the culture in which one is raised has an impact, Northrup is convinced that this is outweighed many times over by the influence of our individual mothers. The relationship with our mothers can be powerful, passionate and intimate. At the same time mothers and daughters are able to disappoint and hurt each other in no small measure. The unprocessed fears, the pain and grief of our mothers and all our maternal ancestors are part of our heritage and thus part of the relationship we have with them.

> 'Some call me the girl who was shot by the taliban, or the girl who fought for her rights. However, my brothers still call me that annoying bossy sister. I am just a commited, even stubborn person who wants to see every child to have equal rights and peace everywhere.'
> — MALALA YOUSAFZAI Nobel Peace Prize acceptance speech on *YouTube*

In one of the workshops on the Eldest Daughter Day we asked the question: 'What are the most important relationships within your family and how would you draw them?' It did not take long for the conversation to start on the relationship with the mother, which did not always prove to be straightforward and simple. 'She holds norms that are not mine and when I find myself living up to them, I start to lose my sense of self,' one participant said. 'I feel I never quite live up to her expectations,' another one stated, adding: 'She expects so much from me that I am paralyzed before I begin.' A third one felt immensely responsible for the well-being of her mother, which got in the way of a truly open relationship with her.

On the other hand, a number of eldest daughters were flabbergasted at these comments. They did not recognize those sorts of interactions at all as they and their mothers had always been very close. They felt or feel notably safe with their mother and have an open easy dialogue with her about many aspects of their lives. This goes to show that while we might recognize each other on a deep level, our lives and relationships can still be markedly different.

## Handing down

Whether your relationship with your mother is easy, intimate or complicated, you are an intermediary. Everything that you as a baby or child have been through still lives within you and will be passed down to your children, whether you are aware of it or not. Was your mother an eldest or was she the baby of the family? How did she get along with her own mother? Only when you have figured out why your mother is the way she is can you begin to recognize certain behaviours of hers and adjust your response. You may not be able to change your mother but you can change your own perception of her. Especially if your relationship is currently problematic, you will be able to comprehend better why she acts the way she does when you can put yourself in her shoes. It can often be quite healing to realize that, in the circumstances, your mother did the best she could.

Northrup describes the need for women to realize that they carry the blueprint of all previous generations within. When she works with groups of women, she often has them begin by speaking aloud the names of their mother, maternal grandmother and great-grandmother. Often tears are shed. Speaking the names of the women you hail from opens up the indestructible ties that exist with your own mother and all those before her in your family line. Pain may come to the surface that may not even be your own. Northrup is not the only one who is convinced that being aware of the deep-running roots of the female line helps you be a better mum.

Becoming conscious of your role as a parent is something that grows on you. Parental love is not only strong, it is also an extremely vulnerable kind of love. Anything that happens to your baby, your child, goes straight to your heart. By acknowledging what happens to you in each new situation and witnessing how your child responds, you are given the opportunity to deepen your self-awareness. If you are courageous enough to look into your relationship with your own mother and come to grips with it, you provide your daughter with the best chance of an emotionally and physically healthy life.

## The first phase

However well-intentioned parents are, they will inevitably make mistakes. Also, this is just the way it is: parents learn through trial and error and the firstborn is their guinea pig. In *The Birth Order Book* Kevin Leman states that the chances are that parents who are firstborns themselves will make considerable demands of their own firstborn. They identify so much with their eldest that they hold them to the same high level of expectations as themselves. Since this is their first time operating as parents, in truth they have no clue what they can hope for. While children on average make their first baby steps at twelve months, firstborn parents will probably try to stimulate their infant to do this at eleven months, even if the child is not ready. Experienced parents know that children will walk when they walk. According to Kevin Leman, a mother who is a firstborn herself will unknowingly push her eldest just a bit more than she will her other children.

All experts agree that it is wise to pay attention to how eagerly your firstborn tries to be exactly like you, her Mummy. When you give her an approving smile and encourage her with words of praise, her sense of safety is strengthened. So with heart and soul she will try to hold your attention by mimicking you and trying her best. This poses the risk of her attempting to be a kind of mini-adult, because at her young age how can she possibly do things as well as her parents? This is mission impossible. It goes without saying that it is fine to give your daughter a lot of attention – of course you'll want to stimulate and encourage her in her development – but spurring her on too much may lead to her feeling that she is always falling short, never quite good enough.

Another hazard is that parents can project their own unfulfilled dreams onto their eldest daughter, even when they are aware of doing so. 'We are so proud of our firstborn. She just has so many talents.'

Having stomached our share of disappointments in life, it can be tempting to expect her to make good on what you had always wanted to achieve. If this makes her happy, then all is well. In her autobiography *Yesterday, Today, Tomorrow*, the Italian movie star and icon Sophia Loren who, late in her long career, received the Academy Award for her contribution to world cinema, stresses that she would never have achieved what she did without her mother Romilda. She was the one who dragged her naive eldest daughter to a beauty pageant. The woman who would make a fortune with her talent and beauty describes how they barely had enough money to eat but her 'Mammina' was not going to let this opportunity slip away. Her own chance had been denied to her by her parents, and she'd never forgotten it. As a good eldest daughter Sophia submitted to her mother's will the way she usually did. She was not quite old enough to enter the pageant, but her mother twisted her hair up to make her look more mature, and threw herself wholeheartedly into the job of preparing her firstborn for the big event.

In the case of La Loren this turned out well, but eldest daughters may be pleasers who push their own boundaries so they can continue to be the good girl. As a parent of an eldest daughter, it is good to be aware of whether a choice is genuinely hers or whether she is just complying to keep you happy.

## Source of concern

Strange as it may seem, this first child who you are so inordinately proud of may also turn out to be the one who causes you the most concern. You worry about her, maybe because you recognize so much of yourself in her. You comprehend the fears and insecurities that may haunt her. It is as if you see yourself in the mirror that she holds up to you. More than her younger siblings she will require your appreciation and support, because she wants so badly to excel. As an eldest daughter turned mother, you may find yourself in a fix. You will want to shield your child from the notion that improvement is the key to happiness and that she perpetually has to do better, because you know so well how that feels. You want her to realize that you adore her as much as you do the cute little sister or brother. That you love her for who she is and not for how well she performs. In that regard, insight into how to compliment a child comes in handy. There is a difference between appreciating her for something she did well: 'Your room is nice and tidy' and something that is sometimes called false praise, such as: 'You are the sweetest and cleverest girl in the world because you tidied up so well.' She is better off knowing that your love for her has nothing to do with how well she behaves.

> *'I've got two daughters who will have to make their way in this skinny-obsessed world, and it worries me, because I don't want them to be empty-headed, self-obsessed, emaciated clones; I'd rather they were independent, interesting, idealistic, kind, opinionated, original, funny – a thousand things before "thin". Let my girls be Hermiones.'*
>
> —— J.K. ROWLING in blog *For Girls Only, Probably*

Sometimes the eldest is a source of concern because she tends to be a worrier herself. Her ingrained sense of responsibility has her agonizing about 'the little ones', or whether you as parents are sticking it out and how Grandmother will survive after Grandfather's passing. As her world expands, so do her causes for anxiety. She worries about what is on the evening news. One mother told the story of what usually happens when she comes home from work. Her thirteen-year-old sits in the living room with a somewhat dejected look. When she asks how her day has been, the reply is no more than a slight introverted shrug. Then the two younger ones come running in the door, full of stories and things to show her. 'Frequently I just leave the eldest be because I am having such a good time with the other two. Of course, I try to draw her in but I hardly ever succeed. She cannot grasp that we are not bogged down by the suffering in the world and we are not prepared to allow her to spoil our good mood.'

This situation may not apply to each and every eldest daughter; there are certainly those of us who are easy-going – but it is a fact that the sense of responsibility and the solicitousness of the eldest often brings its share of apprehension. Add the typical thoughtful approach and you have a child who takes the worries of the world on her shoulders. This need not only be the case during adolescence, when the eyes open more widely to what occurs outside of the first small circle of care. The engagement with what happens to others may also be a decisive factor in the choice of education and career that an eldest daughter pursues.

### What about the father?

The story of the father and the daughter was and still is that of the hero and the princess. Classic psychoanalytical theory has it that the girl falls in love with her dad. He cannot marry her, but he can protect her and prepare her for life in the harsh world out there. Ordinarily he will do so with a vengeance as nothing touches him deeper than the tiny, vulnerable baby girl he held in his arms when she was born. She will be the princess he throws up in the air with her fully trusting him to catch her safely. Talking to eldest daughters we have noticed that regardless of their age and what they have achieved in their lives, the heroic-father notion is generally alive and kicking.

With the father there is no issue of identification. This is reserved for the mother, with whom a girl naturally identifies and thus from whom she has to disengage herself – with some daughters going out of their way not to resemble their mothers. The father is special. During the Eldest Daughter Day women spoke of how their fathers showed their pride in them so much more easily than did their mothers. They went fishing with their dad, out on long walks or adventurous trips where she could show him how tough she could be and he could take pride in her. The eldest daughters also confessed to one another how they twisted him around their little finger. In retrospect they saw that on occasion they had imagined themselves taking their mother's place, especially when their mother could for some reason not totally fulfil her role as carer or partner. To this day, they said, when something needed to be arranged for the whole family, they preferred to handle it with their father. Some of them had followed in his footsteps, learned the tricks of his trade and thus have a common topic of conversation with him for the rest of their lives. He remained their source of inspiration, the man they hold in the highest regard, the one who they perennially want to show how good they have become.

Birth order plays a significant role in forging this extra-strong bond between father and eldest daughter. With the mother, especially initially, fully occupied with the care of number two, the eldest often turns to the father. The mother might inadvertently stimulate this new fellowship. 'Why don't you take her with you so I have my hands free for the little one?' she says, and the eldest daughter happily skips to her dad. She may hurt a little from her mother evidently preferring to spend time with the baby; yet she feels flattered that her father likes to take her along. She adores him and wants to stay special to him for ever and ever.

Fathers treat their children differently from mothers. When their daughters climb a tree, they call out: Higher! This toughens up their daughter, makes her sturdier. She in turn likes playing with her dad. Especially when her mother says they should be careful and he just continues. Moments like that make her feel the bond with her father even more strongly as there is a pact from which her mother is excluded. The ensuing sense of self-worth makes her turn to him even more. The desire to please him with good behaviour, high grades and, later, a challenging job so he can be proud of her for evermore, may long serve as a strong motivation for an eldest daughter.

Science reporter Paul Raeburn wanted to find scientific evidence of the importance of a father in the lives of his offspring. In his book *Do Fathers Matter?*, published in 2014, he shows that fathers exert a much larger educational influence on their children than is often assumed. Emotionally as well as physically, fathers may have a big impact on the health of their children. Even if they have no inkling that this is happening, fathers-to-be go through all kinds of hormonal changes when their partner is pregnant. Raeburn wants to reassure fathers of their significance, show them that they need to be around from the very first moment. Such conscious fathers will also be more willing to get out of bed in the night to comfort the baby. They are 'the new fathers'. Of course, they will also want to pay extra attention to their eldest daughters when a second child arrives. These days, however, patterns are not so strict and mothers are increasingly likely to be the main breadwinner while many fathers take on the role of full-time carers.

> *'If you have an eldest daughter for a mother, there is less need to be such an eldest daughter yourself.'*
> —— ELDEST DAUGHTER during the *Eldest Daughter Day*

## I'll be different

Almost everyone recognizes the idea that you are going to handle parenthood very differently from your parents. Better, of course. Regardless of how your relationship with your mother is, for your own eldest daughter you want to be the very best.

When your young daughter displays a tendency to take responsibility for her younger brother or sister, then as a mother you can interfere. You don't want her carrying that heavy load, even if you have to admit she would be up to it. If your parents always encouraged or expected you to be the eldest and the wisest, chances are that you don't want to lay that burden on your own firstborn. If you yourself had to do a lot of practical tasks within the household at a tender age, taking care of your siblings, packing their lunch and getting them into their coats, you will wish your own daughter to have a carefree youth. You don't want to turn her into a babysitter.

At some point during the Eldest Daughter Day a sigh of relief went through the audience as a young woman, who had come with her mother, shared that she could not connect to the heavier, more responsible aspects of being the eldest at all. Her mother had shielded her. This turned out to have been the objective of many mothers in the room. Isn't it a pleasant surprise that your own experience as an eldest daughter works to your advantage now that you are a mother yourself?

One of the pitfalls for young girls is the belief that they are responsible for the well-being of everyone else. This assumption puts them in an impossible spot as a child, and later in life, because it prohibits them from gauging what they themselves feel and want. Keeping others happy seemed more important to their young selves than finding out what made them tick. When as an eldest you are aware of this snag, you are especially likely to make sure that your daughter learns to go her own way. You will try to ensure that she is not solely governed by her sense of duty, thoughtfulness and responsible attitude. These are, of course, wonderful qualities but they may also keep you away from the whispers of your heart and your intuition.

> *'I am beyond thrilled to introduce you to our Max. Her being fills us with hope and inspires us to join others in creating a better future.'*
>
> — PRISCILLA CHAN ZUCKERBERG on *Facebook*

Even if we are well aware of how we want to go about things, life may turn out differently. Experts in the field of childrearing know that there is always a discrepancy between theory and practice. Although as a mother of an eldest daughter you are convinced that you don't want to saddle her with tasks that are not what she enjoys, at some point you might do so anyway. During the Eldest Daughter Day a young mother shared how she assigns her daughter small tasks. When another woman asked if she wasn't giving her daughter a responsibility that she actually should not have, the young mother reacted with surprise. She had never thought twice about what she was doing and hadn't even noticed the very pattern she had wanted to avoid.

The same thing happened to Wies, whose eldest daughter Didi is now a grown woman. When Wies said that she had been very mindful in preventing her daughter taking on too much responsibility at a young age, Didi laughed and gave an example that stopped Wies in her tracks. She had completely forgotten about the incident in the swimming pool, the moment Didi leapt into the water because her younger sister had fallen in and apparently no one else was paying attention. Didi had acted without a moment's hesitation. The sense of being responsible had already been instilled. Wies argued that she has not treated Didi differently from her younger sister, but her eldest daughter remained unconvinced. She reminded her mother of the fact that she always had to perform well at school, because she had the intelligence. Wies had to concede that the high level of pressure she had exerted on her was indeed different from the more lax attitude she had displayed towards her younger daughter. Through Didi, the eldest, Wies, like so many other mothers, had figured out that things usually work out fine if you let them be. The baby of the family had benefitted from the experience gained with the firstborn. Point taken, Wies said.

### Training on the job

Raising children is a craft that you learn by doing. No one will deny that the eldest has a mother who is least experienced and who, yes, makes mistakes. We know that a majority of eldest daughters would do anything to avoid getting even the tiniest thing wrong, but it is only normal that as a mother you don't always respond to your child as perfectly as you would like. Perfect mothers don't exist; you become a mother suddenly, but also over time. There is no harm in doing some self-reflection, for instance on the level of perfection that you demand of your daughter. How do you perceive her? What does she see when she looks into your eyes? Fear? Worry? Disappointment? Love? Understanding? The more you as the mother become conscious of the patterns running through eldest daughters, the more unlikely it is that you will demand of her that she be 'the perfect eldest'; you will realize that there is as little chance of her being this as there is of you being the perfect mother.

Never forget that your eldest daughter is an individual born in a different time and a different family to that in which you were born. Much has changed in the meantime. You may safely assume that she has everything within her to lead a good life, if you grant her the right to make the mistakes she needs to make. What she needs most is the certainty that whatever happens, you love her deeply.

## IN BRIEF

- As a woman you carry a blueprint of motherhood within you.
- Contemplating the relationship with your own mother is important for the relationship with your own eldest daughter.
- A firstborn wants to imitate and copy her parents the best she can; pointing out how she can do better might sow the seeds of perfectionism in her.
- The role of the father is still undervalued.
- Your own experience as an eldest is of great benefit in your role as mother.

# 11.

# The ongoing family dance

• • •

**LISETTE**  Twice recently I proposed to my mother and siblings that we should go visit our youngest brother. He has been living in the United States longer than he lived in the Netherlands, where he was born and the rest of us are based. The first time I hatched this plan was for his fiftieth birthday in January. 'Why don't we pay him a surprise visit?' I said. 'The timing doesn't work for me,' my other brother muttered. My sister had to reschedule a few business meetings and when we made our travel plans, our 86-year-old mother was eager to join us on this transatlantic trip. My brother, too, in the end.

Wordlessly we divided the tasks. I kept in touch with my American brother's new partner – for our brother himself, we'd decided our visit was to be a surprise. My brother booked the hotel and a car big enough to fit us all. My sister made the arrangements for my mother to be able to travel with us. In the early hours of the day of departure I found the two of them at a coffee stand at Amsterdam Schiphol Airport; my brother had already gone to the gate. On the plane he was not seated with us either. Once in the US, he was happy to drive us to the hotel that he had picked. Quickly we changed out of our travel clothes into something more festive and walked through the snow to the designated restaurant. My mother went in first. My youngest brother looked at her. Not believing his eyes, he looked again and then, of course, we all started crying. With the physical distance between us, my brother's young children don't know us very well but they still wanted to sit on our laps right away. At eight o'clock (which would have been two a.m. at home) my mother was still radiant in the company of her youngest son, whom she insists on calling' 'her baby'.

We spent a few days together, rehashing old jokes, teasing each other in familiar ways, fondly singing the same old songs we know by heart. It struck me how easily the three of us, who grew up together until our youngest brother arrived, are inclined to meddle in his life. Unashamedly we ask him all kinds of questions that we would not dream of asking one another, and we don't hold back in our criticism. It is as if we look down upon his life from somewhere up high and shamelessly stir it with a stick, much like a child does to an ants' nest. My youngest brother defends himself. 'Life is different here,' he says. 'You don't understand.'

In August of the same year he suddenly announced that he was getting married. The stars were favourable according to his future bride. 'Let's go over,' I said. 'The timing doesn't work for me,' my other brother muttered. Then he realized he could fit in a stop to see his youngest daughter who was studying in the United States for a semester. My sister and her husband were game, too, and my mother was delighted at the opportunity to be with all of us once more. I hunted for a present. My brother booked the hotel and the car. My sister made the arrangements for my mother. While there, my siblings took it for granted that I would give a speech. I was delighted. They knew. We've known each other our whole lives.

## Into the world

Blanche, a thirty-something entrepreneur in the arts, had stayed living at home for a year longer than she had wanted to, she told us on the Eldest Daughter Day. She did this for her mother who was not yet ready to give up her daily company. She also did this for the sister thirteen years her junior who regards her as a second mother. But finally the time came to leave; she had to spread her wings, find her own way in the world and become who she is. She still joins them for dinner each Sunday night. She listens to the stories of these two people who are so dear to her heart, and goes back to the place that is her own home now, the place from which she can uncouple herself from the family in which she will forever remain the eldest.

You can leave home but home never quite leaves you. The written and unwritten rules of engagement that are slightly different in each family, the role you played as the eldest in the birth order and the way you have shaped one another as parents and children have become an integral part of you. You will remain inextricably linked to the people with whom you grew up. You have gone through so much together, you share so many memories, so many jokes that still make you laugh after all these years. Friends or in-laws are astounded – and slightly bored sometimes – when the same old story about an otherworldly cousin or eccentric aunt is being repeated yet again.

This is not about the content; everyone knows exactly what is coming. Stories about the good old days strengthen the sense of being allies; the repetition serves as an affirmation of the shared history that only the ones who were there truly comprehend. Nobody else but the ones with whom you lived under one roof for so many years grasps precisely how family life at your place used to be. Even the children of the neighbours or really good childhood friends who came over on a daily basis don't have the full picture. Both the bad and the good from everyday existence – who used to monopolize the shower, what made your mother lose her temper, why you used to go to the same holiday destination over and over again or how your father fried the eggs on Sunday morning – you can never fully spell these things out to someone else.

Only between those who grew up together does a half word tell what you mean when you allude to such situations. Sometimes you share the same memories; at other times what you remember from days gone by and situations you shared may be dissimilar. Yet in your bones you feel what you have been party to and still are, even if your lives may have turned out very differently once you all left the family home. The eldest daughter is often the first one to take the plunge. She needs to take a step into the unknown and make her way, thus serving as an example to those who come after her. This is, moreover, a step that will inevitably emphasize the difference from those who still live at home.

Differentiation is needed in order to stand on your own two feet. While siblings belong together, they are not the same, which is a clear fact of life when growing up. Aside from the unmistakable impact of the birth order, there are differences in temperament and pace, in intelligence and interests, between the girls and the boys. Some families allow for more variation than others where everyone is more or less treated in the same fashion. Whichever was the preferred modus operandi in your family, it is only when you start out on your own that you will discover the huge effect it has had on you. Things you have always thought were self-evident turn out, for others, not to be that way at all. This may be evident in the way you handle money, for instance, what you like to eat at what time or whether you screw the cap back on to the toothpaste tube or not. New friends offer fresh perspectives and unfamiliar customs. By trial and error you will discover your own way of life. You are now free to take a stand on issues small and big. What approach do you want to take to existence? What fits you best?

In order to find their own answers to the manifold questions life poses, one person may need more distance than the next one. On the Eldest Daughter Day, Emily, now in her late forties, admitted that it had taken her a long time before she was able to form her own opinions. Her mother suffered from severe depressions and, as the eldest, Emily had taught herself first and foremost to keep quiet. She made it a habit not to voice her opinions or speak of her feelings. Don't rock the boat. Only after she had become conscious of the degree to which she had convinced herself that what she thought or felt didn't matter, did she slowly gather the courage to offer her own point of view.

Other eldest daughters confessed that they had long voted for the same political candidates as their parents. No one would suspect from looking at these competent women that the realization that they had a vote and a voice of their own had only dawned on them gradually. Even a woman like Madeleine Albright, who became America's Secretary of State, admits that it took her quite a long time to develop a voice. She did add, 'And now that I have it, I am not going to be silent.'

## Letting go and staying close

Eldests often remain loyal to their family for a long time. Some are only able to forge a life of their own by consciously creating a rift for a while. Maria, who comes from a large family, felt at the time that as the eldest she was expected to be available for and take care of her younger siblings for the rest of her life. She drew a line in the sand when she left home and took refuge in her job in the social sector. In this way she was still a caretaker, but on her own terms and without any contact with her family. 'I hated to have to be so harsh. It felt like I was fleeing, but back then I did not see another way of escaping the expectations of my family,' she says now.

> *'It takes a great deal of courage and independence to decide to design your own image instead of the one that society rewards, but it gets easier as you go along.'*
>
> —— GERMAINE GREER in *The Female Eunuch*

Just as in any other relationship there are four distinct ways to become yourself vis-à-vis the ones closest to you: being compliant, rebelling, going on the offensive or creating a rift. A compliant eldest daughter will slowly crawl out from under her parents' wings, hoping all the time that no one notices that she is starting to do things differently. When she is at home, she pretends that she has not changed at all, as if she is not growing and developing in her own way. A rebel will choose the opposite and delight in doing things completely differently, experimenting while the family hold their breath and pray that their impetuous child will soon find her own middle ground.

The third way is that of the frontal attack. A headstrong young adult can do this openly by protesting vigorously against the customary ways, or inwardly in silence. In either case she will paint an inner picture of her parents as wardens who intend to keep her small. Such a story can develop quite a momentum of its own. Inwardly she will fight these stern parents, which may manifest in a kind of permanent state of irritation. She'll become a testy, touchy person who the others in the family tend to avoid provoking. The anger that arose at the time of the birth of the second child may be a subconscious source of this fretful state. The fourth method is the one Maria applied: take a break, be out of touch for a while or for some people, even cut the ties and find out who you are and what kind of life is hidden within you away from the family situation.

Many eldest daughters mix the above strategies. They may, for instance, choose to take the educational path that makes sense according to their father, and thus appear to remain the good girl that he is accustomed to, only to come home with a partner who doesn't fit the bill at all. Others may consciously pull back from the family dynamic. They move away to another town or another state and don't attend all the family celebrations. From a safe distance they may continue to be the ideal eldest in the minds of their parents, while actually leading an unobserved life of their own.

Family is like a dance-floor where the dancers perpetually take new steps, crash into one another and have to find, and sometimes capture, space for their own expression. Each time one of the family members changes a bit, brings home a new person or claims some privacy for a while, the whole system needs to adjust and find a new balance. The dance, however, continues. Whether family members are in touch or not, they do keep tabs on one another. 'While all of us are over forty, I am still attentive to see if my siblings fare well,' one of the eldest daughters said and the others nodded their recognition.

### Old roles

From the first screen test she saw, J.K. Rowling was adamant: she wanted Emma Watson to play the role of the clever Hermione. The author of the Harry Potter books and the actress are both eldest daughters. Maybe this is what they recognized in one another. In eight movies within ten years, as an audience we have been witness to Watson's development into an accomplished actress. The moment the movie series came to an end, she went for a haircut. Pictures of her graced the covers of *Elle* magazine and *Teen Vogue*. Pictures of her as herself. However, everyone who sees her photo still cannot help thinking of Hermione – who incidentally was meant to have a younger sibling, but J.K. Rowling later decided to let go of that idea, so that this responsible, dutiful, hands-on know-it-all character remained an only child. For long years to come, whatever films Emma Watson may star in, reviews will still mention that first role she played.

Roles are extremely strong and persistent, and this does not just apply to actresses. Visiting your parents or giving them a call, you will feel how the role you once played within the family is apt to creep up on you again. You may have changed in the meantime, have grown, become yourself, become someone of importance in the outside world, but as soon as you re-enter the family situation, something odd happens. It is almost as if you step into a Harry Potter movie yourself; whether you like it or not, you shrink a little. You shrink until you fit back into the role you always took. This may take five seconds, five minutes or five hours, but then you are squarely back in the familiar old mould. There's nothing you can do about it. You will speak out a bit too vehemently and too fast about something in the life of the youngest; without thinking you will take the lead in organizing the party to celebrate your parents' wedding anniversary. The others let you do your thing. Just like you, they are back in their customary roles, too.

However well you have got to know each other over the years, you will never quite know how the others have interpreted their youthful experiences. You may try, but as the eldest you will never truly be able to fathom how it is to have been born after you, to always have someone else walking in front of you on the path of life. You will never know how it was to read books you had finished long ago, be given the coat that had looked so good on you, meet the teachers who were used to you always having your homework done. As the eldest, you only know how it is to have siblings below you. That is, when your parents stay together.

## Blended families

Seven-year-old Aisa was at a loss to answer the question of whether she was the eldest. Yes, she was her mother's eldest daughter and her brother's eldest sister, but from an earlier marriage her father has four children, so she is a middle child as well. For her this is a situation she has grown up with and always known. Ann, however, was in her mid-twenties when her mother's second marriage provided her with an elder brother and sister. She continues to feel like the eldest sister of her own sisters, she says. 'There is an advantage, too, to having elder siblings all of a sudden. I am really curious how they are dealing with getting a job, a partner and children. It takes the heat off me now that my mother is also concerned with their future.'

Even in this day and age, most parents stick together and thus their children remain in the same spot within the family order their whole lives. Still, many marriages end in divorce and with the number of unmarried people having children, too, statistics are less and less trustworthy regarding how many children grow up in either one-parent or composite families. The UN's Demographics and Social Statistics Division keeps track of the ratio of marriages to divorces worldwide, and the statistics demonstrate that certain nationalities are significantly more likely to get divorced than others.

The social acceptance of divorce in a country may in part contribute to this, as indeed may the ease and expense with which a divorce can be carried out. While countries such as Jamaica, Colombia and Mexico all have comparatively low levels of divorce, some ostensibly traditional nations report surprisingly high rates. It is well reported that over half of all marriages in the United States end in divorce. With such a high population that is an awful lot of household break-ups: one every six seconds, in fact. And, perhaps predictably, the more often you marry, the more likely you are to go through another divorce: seventy-three per cent of third marriages in the United States don't last.

Many European countries have an even higher divorce rate. Again according to the UN's Demographics and Social Statistics Division, Belgium heads the list of marriages falling to pieces with a staggering seventy-three per cent, followed by Portugal, Hungary, Czech Republic, Spain, Luxembourg, Estonia, Cuba and France and the US in tenth place. It has long been thought that only one parent could properly raise the children after a marital break-up and thus the other parent was usually given visiting rights only. Nowadays, however, parents are more inclined to shoulder responsibility for their offspring together and in many instances legislation starts to follow suit. In such cases the child is no longer brought into the impossible and traumatizing situation of needing to choose one parent over the other. Living in two houses alternately, they can have meaningful relationships with both, if they are willing to, of course. When one of the parents enters into a new relationship with someone who already has children of their own, the families are stitched together. The impact of this occurrence depends in a large measure on the age at which it happens.

> *'Nobody but you is responsible for your life. What is your life? What is every flower, every rock, every tree? Energy. And you're responsible for the energy you create for yourself, and you're responsible for the energy that you bring to others.'*
>
> —— OPRAH WINFREY on *The Oprah Winfrey Show*

Judy Dunn, professor of developmental psychology at King's College in London, has found that children as young as three who are raised with step- or half-siblings are already aware of who belongs to their genetic family and who doesn't. She also found that this distinction becomes less great the longer that siblings with different parents live, play, eat, talk, fight and make up together. A long-term American investigation of 720 families showed that with each year that passes there is less and less to distinguish the dynamics within a blended family from those of a nuclear family. After six years, on average, differences seem to disappear altogether. The bonds formed between children from different marriages during that six-year period are unlikely to be broken.

Of course, not all children spend those six years at home; thus it may be that the ties forged are much stronger between the younger children who grow up together, while the eldest has already left home before the six-year period is over. She continues with her life without being given the time to develop day-to-day intimacy and closeness with her new siblings. No one has yet taken up the challenge of studying the effect of blending families and its impact on the birth order line-up. 'We don't actually have a way of quantifying it,' says Frank Sulloway, the acknowledged leader of research in this field. 'Whatever disrupts a family also disrupts the family niches and thus predictions based on birth order.'

Divorce can cast long shadows and many will experience tension even imagining their parents together, for instance at their wedding. It takes a lot of work for parents to get beyond their emotions and allow healing to happen, as Dr Christiane Northrup shares in a personal story on her website. When her youngest daughter Kate asked her to create a women-only blessing ceremony, Northrup consciously included Kate's stepmother and twelve-year-old stepsister in the circle. 'Heaven knows,' she writes, 'we can all use as many mothers – and blessings – as we can get.'

What seemed to come as a surprise was that this wedding brought healing for herself as well. After the vows, Kate's dad spontaneously took her hand and said, 'This is a day of endings and new beginnings. And I so look forward to including you in the new beginning.' Later that evening his young daughter, whom Northrup had met only once before, put her arms round her waist and asked, 'How are we related?' Northrup's eldest daughter, Annie, told her, 'She's your bonus mom.' That instant the circle of the family widened for all of them. 'I want to acknowledge you for all the work you've done around your own heart,' her youngest daughter wrote to her a few days after the wedding, adding, 'to be able to enjoy this time free of worry about any tension between you and Dad or around the blending of families is the biggest gift.'

## The care conundrum

When all siblings have left home and built lives of their own, the one place you generally see each other is at your parents'. They remain the intersection where the various roads meet. In some families there is a weekly coffee klatsch at the weekend; others meet only at holidays, weddings, significant birthdays or anniversaries. Traditionally, everyone is primarily kept up to date on the others' lives through the mother. She is usually the hub where everyone's information is gathered and, whatever she knows, she shares with the others – it is not uncommon that she does this without holding anything back, happily divulging secrets without any censorship. Between siblings the conversation may often be about the one who isn't present at the time, or about the aging parents who need more care as time goes on. Who is going to take that on? Maybe the youngest lives close by and is able to fulfil this task. A brother who is not particularly good at caregiving might take over the family administration from the aging father. Very often, however, it is the caring, responsible, dutiful eldest daughter who becomes the primary caretaker of one or both parents.

We interviewed Marga Jacobs, a clinical psychologist and psychotherapist who works with people over sixty in her practice: Recently she began to notice similarities in the issues reported by a number of her female clients. When there was no one left to take care of, or when they couldn't handle the care for someone else due to their own physical condition, all these women had fallen into a sort of limbo. They proved to be stubbornly set in their behavioural patterns, and wanted only to go back to the past and to the way things were. 'As a therapist I always ask older people about their past and their position in the birth order,' Jacobs says.

She does this by making a genogram, a kind of family tree that shows how the family is made up. 'Without exception these women turned out to be eldest daughters. They tended to consider their father more like a friend who had to be protected, or they had an absent father. They often have a complex and complicated relationship with their mothers. Yet these eldest daughters continue to take care of her at an advanced age, even when the mother doesn't appreciate it at all. In an extreme case an eldest daughter kept coming to care for a mother who used to spit at her. I am talking about women who have been engaged to do part of the household work at a young age. Sometimes they have had to come home after having left to obtain an education, to help out at home or to mediate between their parents.'

Jacobs refers to women who were born in or before the nineteen-fifties, a completely different day and age. We've had women's liberation since then, and individualism, but with state budgets shrinking there is still a good deal of the duty of care that comes back to women, and more often than not this will mean the eldest daughter.

The sunny side of the care conundrum is that these women are forces of nature. 'They are on the receiving end of a lot of appreciation,' Jacobs says. 'The thing is: this only makes it harder to stop doing what they're doing. Many eldest daughters need to discover throughout their lives that they should not only take care of others but of themselves as well. Many, of course, succeed in doing this but those who don't manage to get around to self-care are bound to fall into the aforementioned limbo. Loneliness lurks around the corner when they grow older: contacts grow increasingly difficult as others feel patronized by someone who wants to take care of them all the time. For many, this compulsive caring has created a rift with their brothers and sisters. In my sessions with them I propose to change these fixed patterns. Often I find they first need to receive praise for their sustained efforts before they can even hear questions like: "What is your self-image and what do you do with your feelings? How long have you been craving acknowledgement and acceptation? What is the price you have paid for being so caring? Do you ask for help yourself, do you give others a chance to be there for you? What do you want?" That last question often takes them by surprise. "What do I want?" they wonder. "Just for my children to be happy," is an answer many of them give. I used the topic for a talk when I had first discovered this pattern among eldest daughters. Someone in the audience asked if I was an eldest daughter myself. It sounds weird but it had not occurred to me that I am one. For me, too, it is hard not to assume the role of caregiver. Many of us have been doing this for so long that we don't even notice but it is important to stop taking this for granted. When you can reconsider volunteering to take something on that in actual fact you can't or don't want to do, a whole new life begins.'

## A rubber band

The bond with the people you grew up with is like an elastic band. It can stretch quite a way. You may go and live on the other side of the world and yet, you still belong unconditionally. When something bad happens, the rubber band pulls you back home. Skype has its uses but sometimes you need to be able to hold one another, celebrate together or merely sit in the same room without needing to say much because there just isn't much to say. You are aware of what each of you is feeling at moments like that: at an important birthday or a wedding, when a child is born, a relationship has broken up or someone falls seriously ill. These are all moments when family, however little you see of each other in your daily lives, is all of a sudden prominent. These are not people you have chosen to be in your life; they just are, and all through the years you have lived with their peculiarities, just as they have with yours. You know each other's favourite dishes and songs, each other's weak spots and strengths, you know each other through and through.

There is an intimacy that stems from the way your parents raised you. In the formative years of your youth you had to make do with these people whose lives coincided with yours. In the inevitable sibling rivalry you've fought your battles. Who won the ping-pong tournaments, who was the first to dare to jump off the high board? As the eldest you wanted to be first and best; the others were eager to trump you. In manifold ways you co-developed. Sometimes through harsh opposition, and still these days you may find yourself locking horns with your sister or brother. You burst out when you hadn't meant to or the other way round; you feel pummelled by one of them in a way that completely upsets you. Sensitive spots remain tender and at the same time you are well aware of who you are dealing with. Maybe you would avoid a friend after such a collision, but a brother or sister remains in your life, even if you decide to keep your distance for a while. This is a common occurrence in all families. Even when you do remain close, there are subjects better left unaddressed in return for smooth sailing. For the sake of this smooth sailing, perhaps you had better not start a discussion on politics but instead tell a story about a movie you've recently seen – and before you know it you'll be harking back to the posters of stars you had on your bedroom walls and you are back on common ground.

Through the rough and the smooth the relationship with your siblings is the longest of your life, longer even than the one with your parents and or with your own children. As an adult you can now make the choice that was made for you when you were a child: do you give your siblings access to your inner life or would you rather keep to yourself? Do you restrict your visits to birthdays and other family events or do you consciously add a measure of friendship to the family tie? Being close to one or more of your siblings may bring enormous richness to your life. As one of the women we interviewed for our research said: 'My sister was born a year and a half after me. She married a year and a half after me, had her first child a year and a half after me. We go through life together, arm in arm.' The protective arm that you may have thrown round your younger sister or brother on the sofa or at school – who does not have that typical sibling photograph? The age difference that was so huge when you were small no longer plays a role once you are grown-ups; while at the same time you never fully forget who is the eldest and who is the youngest.

## The time has come

When someone in the family dies, the most intimate circle gathers close. Most of us are acutely aware of the various circles the ailing person has around them and when the time comes, only the innermost circle will attend. In some families, even the partners of brothers and sisters may be too much at some points. When push comes to shove the people you grew up with turn out to be the most important ones. The long lines of the shared history in which you have come to know one another, to the bone, are what count; the memories of moments when you may have been mortified or laughed till you cried. This bond for life now has a life of its own. Those are the people you want close by when you are touched to the core. Even the person you never really got along with so well – the hatchet is buried now. While death will take away from you the one whose time has come, it is also death that tightly binds those remaining. Now all that matters is to surround the dear dying one with love or to pay your loving respects. Each family member plays their part in the procedure. Ideally, you can give each other space and be kind when one of you for a moment cannot deal with things; one of you may attempt to lighten the mood with humour.

Finally, there you are in your mother or father's obituary notice, your names in the old order of birth, with you, as the eldest daughter, heading the list, the youngest bringing up the rear. You were the first to make your entrance into your parents' lives and so you are the one who has known them the longest. In cases of a large age difference, you have been part of a period of your parents' lives that the youngest only knows from stories. As the eldest, you might consider it a privilege to have had your parents in your life longer than, for instance, a sibling who is ten years younger. This advantage has given you the opportunity to deepen your relationship, heal old wounds and begin to view the people who begot you as who they truly are instead of as just parents. As they aged, the roles you played in society and towards each other have transformed. They retired while you blossomed in your chosen profession and if they lived to a very old age and needed attention and care, maybe you started to feel more like their parent than their child.

Once both your parents are deceased, you, as their brood, have to keep the flame of the family relationships burning. Again, you'll need to find a new balance, a new rhythm in getting together and following what happens in each other's lives. Is it up to you as the eldest to keep everyone united – or have you got to a point where you can see the role but don't necessarily need to take it on? Are you able to accept that someone else within the family is the binding factor rather than you as the eldest? Are you able to share the responsibility for the whole and thus maybe become more part of the family than you have ever been before? Without your father who could make you feel his pride in you, his first child, the apple of his eye, his eldest daughter. Without your mother who loved you unconditionally whether she was able to show you her affection easily or not. You are left with the fellow-travellers of your existence, as one eldest daughter named her brother and sister, the people you have known their whole lives. When something is the matter with them, you will want to know; and vice versa.

Whoopi Goldberg was in London performing in the musical *Sister Act* when her mother suffered a stroke. She rushed back to the United States immediately to be with her family. This was a difficult loss for her and her younger brother. 'My brother and I were very, very lucky to have her in our lives,' she said on *The View*, 'and so I am not sad, because we had a great time.

I think I'm just sad sometimes because I think, "Who will love me the way she did?" But I realized that my brother and I have each other, so we're OK.' Five years later she lost her brother, too.

There is no escaping this fact – one day will be our last. Before that fateful day, you may be close to your siblings physically and emotionally, or more distant, but you are family for ever. Running into one another on the metaphorical family dance-floor, wittingly and unwittingly you will step on each other's toes. While you dance to your own music and claim the space you need, one of the others might make a sudden gesture and hit you hard from left field. You turn in anger, only to find that your sister or brother did not hit you on purpose. Like you, they were just doing their own thing. Their unfortunate move was not directed against you in any way. Do you still need confirmation that the others are not against, but all for you – just as you are unequivocally for them? You give the other a forgiving wink and dance on in your own, undeniably eldest-daughter rhythm.

## IN BRIEF

- Family is like a dance-floor where each of the dancers continually has to find space to express themselves.
- The role you played as first in the birth order and the way, as siblings, you have shaped one another have become part of you.
- You remain inseparably connected to those you grew up with.
- An eldest daughter may need to create some distance in order to come into her own.
- When two families are united through a second marriage, it takes six years of living together for ties to be forged that are as strong as the ones between biological siblings.
- As an adult the eldest has more time than the others to develop a mature relationship with their parents.
- In times of trouble, the elastic band of old draws the family back together again.

# Our research and
# four exercises

We conducted the research for this book by using the Grounded Theory method. Following this relatively new methodology, we did not start off with a hypothesis that we then tried to find evidence for; instead we started by gathering data through conversations with eldest daughters young and old. We then formulated our theory on the basis of what we heard and the patterns we discovered. Working in this way the theory arises out of life itself.

We began with a bang by organizing the Eldest Daughter Day in the spring of 2014. Over one hundred women came from all over the Netherlands, where we are based. From the get-go, they got engaged in open and intimate conversations that were captured by our volunteers – who, of course, were eldest daughters, too. We have used the stacks of information and data that we collected on that day in this book in all kinds of ways. We'd like to note that although we used a scientific model, we don't pretend in any way that we have done a scientific study. We wish to thank Lenneke Aalbers and Pamela van den Berg, who were the creative designers of the programme for that day. We describe four of their exercises below. Thus you can see the basis of our research, and can do these exercises yourself.

## 1. The family web

We all come from families, regardless of their shape or form. From the vantage point of the eldest daughter, how do you see your family members? How do you view others within your wider family who were or still are important to you? This exercise has you discern and name the qualities of the bonds that you have with the various members of your family.

## Step 1

Take a sheet of paper and a pen. Reflect for a moment on the family you hail from and write your own name somewhere on the empty sheet. This is the starting point from which you are going to draw a picture of your family relations. Write the names of your mother and father at the spot they held for you. This might be close to your own name or somewhat further away, the two of them could be close together or have some space between them. Just write their names where you perceive them to be. Then go on to write the names of your sibling(s), again at the spot that seems right to you.

In this way you draw the map of your family. This can, of course, also be a blended family or a foster family. Add family members who were important to you in your youth, even if they are now deceased. Next, jot down the names of loved ones who are in your life now. Draw lines that connect all the people in the drawing with you, and with each other. The result will be a kind of spider's web that has you in the middle and the members of your family and others around you at varying distances.

## Step 2

Once you have drawn the connections between the people in your family, you can focus your attention on the quality of the bonds you feel with them. Take your time in gauging and feeling: how were the relationships with these people for you? What happens when you think of a particular person? Do you frown instantly or do you find yourself smiling? Write one word on every line between you and another person that expresses what this relationship means to you or has meant to you in the past. Add the quality of the bond you feel. This you can mark with smileys, stars, plusses or minuses. You may give points or draw suns and clouds. Do what makes the family relations come alive for you. Remember that this is all from your perspective. How was your own experience of this person in your life? What does she or he mean to you?

## Step 3

Squint for a moment, make your vision blur: what strikes you when you look at your family web in this more abstract way? Does anything in this drawing come as a surprise to you? Imagine you were to give an impression based on this image to someone who is not familiar with your situation. Which family member would you name first? Who would be second? Third? Are you able to put into words why you would proceed in this way?

## Step 4

Now it is time to turn things around. Put yourself in the shoes of the people you have named in your web and ask yourself for a moment how they might see you. How would they define the bond and the relationship with you? Finish, for example, this sentence: what this person is likely to say about me is that I...

## Step 5

Looking at the descriptions you have given about yourself from the point of view of the people in your family web, what do you notice? What are the most important answers for you? What surprises you? Do you see a pattern? What makes you smile? If you were asked to tell a third person how the people close to you perceive you, what would you say? If it could be one word only, what would it be?

## 2. Crucial choices

From a very young age we make choices, small and big. In hindsight, some of these choices tell a story about who we have always been, while others will prove to have been crucial to the way our life turned out. The key with filling in the questionnaire below is not to think too much. Write down the answers fast; just jot down the first thing that comes into your head and take it from there. Doing so may present you with a surprising picture of the choices that have shaped and coloured your life.

## Early youth

- Think back to your first memory of 'holidays' or 'being free from school'. What did you like to do best?
- What did you like to do best when you were at home?
- What was it that you did not like doing but did anyway – maybe to a degree because it was expected of you or because you had to?
- Which member of your family would you have chosen or did you choose to be your favourite? Name a quality or example of what made her or him so special to you.
- Which teacher at school would you say was your favourite? Why?

## Teens to now

- In your teens, who was your best friend? What made this friendship special?
- Who is your best friend now? What makes this friendship special?
- If you could have chosen between school and free time, what would be your choice? What did you like to do best?
- Which kind of clothes did you most like to wear? And what did you not want to wear at all? What did you do when your parents wanted you to change your clothing?
- Who was the teacher/professor you would have chosen as your favourite? What made this person special to you then, and maybe still today?
- If you felt you had to live up to expectations, what were they?
- Who was your first love? How old were you? What happened, what did you do?
- What kind of person did you choose to be your life partner? What is, or was, the story behind this choice? What made this person so significant to you?
- What education/vocation have you chosen or would you have chosen, but didn't? What happened around this choice?

- What was your first job? Was this your own choice? How did you fare with the second – the third?
- What was the hardest choice you've ever had to make in your life?
- What was the most important choice in your life?
- Which choice are you most proud of?

Once you have your list, you may want to look for patterns. What comes as a surprise to you? Where do you feel emotional, and why is that? What would you do differently now, and where do you still need to forgive yourself or others for the choices you made? What choice can you make now that is an expression of the eldest daughter you have become today?

## 3. The key eldest-daughter moment

Some of us have always known that we were the eldest; for others it has been an awareness they've grown into slowly. Others still have suddenly comprehended this fact of life, perhaps because of a radical change in the family situation. How was this for you? What is the key instant for you, the moment when you properly realized you were the eldest daughter? And what was the effect this had on you and your life?

### Step 1

To do this exercise you'll need to use the circles on the following page. Take a pen and look at the circles for a minute. They fan out like ripples in the water when you throw in a stone. Thus, in a while, you may also go from the inside out to find words to describe the moment when you came to realize that you were the eldest. Just sit quietly at first.

Take a deep breath and allow a memory to surface from a time when you grasped more than ever before that you were the eldest daughter. This may be an event from your early youth or a recent occasion at which you truly felt like the firstborn. Describe this realization succinctly in the innermost circle and add your age at the time.

## Step 2

In the next circle briefly state what took place at this point when you grasped you were the eldest daughter. Zoom out a little from yourself to your surroundings. What was happening? Who was present and what contributed to your sudden realization of being the eldest?

The Moment

## Step 3

Now focus on yourself. How was this moment for you? What did you feel? What did you notice inwardly? In the next circle you can describe the feelings and emotions you had at the time. Write down some key words or a phrase that does justice to your inner feelings at that precise moment.

## Step 4

In the outer circle, write down what you said to yourself at the time. What was the lesson you took from that instant; how did you memorize this moment? What was the story you made it into?

## Step 5

Finally, look back with kind and gentle eyes at the girl or the woman you were back then. What would you like to say to her now? What would you like to let her know? Speak from the point of view of who you are now. Write these words in the empty space around the concentric circles. You may want to repeat those words to yourself in the days to come as a loving reminder to who you once were of who you are now.

## 4. Highlighting your qualities

All of us possess talents and qualities, and weaknesses as well. Is it true that there are characteristics that are typical of us, eldest daughters, and that apply to all of us? Good and lesser qualities, ones we are proud of or, conversely, that frustrate us or even evoke a sense of shame? During the Eldest Daughter Day this was one of the explorations we offered to those present. We've integrated the information gained that day into this book. As a reader you may like to do this playful exercise by yourself, but you will gain more insight into yourself – especially your blind spots – if you do it with one or more others. Your partner, your best friend, your children. Whomever you choose, be honest and open. No one is perfect, not even an eldest daughter.

## Step 1

The first step in this exercise is to identify three good qualities that you possess. Take a pen and a piece of paper, or if you have it at hand, three coloured Post-it notes or cards. If you work with blank cards, you may want to put a big plus on one side to mark them as carrying your best qualities. Then go ahead with the three sentences below. Allow some time before you finish them to see what comes to the surface. Don't make this into a thinking project; take what arises spontaneously. Be honest with regard to yourself, even if what arises is pretty positive. There is no need to water it down. Just give an honest reply. You may gain inspiration from letting your eyes dwell on the range of qualities suggested and named during the Eldest Daughter Day; see the list on the next page.

These are the sentences to finish:

- When I am in my element, people often find me…

  _____

- In difficult situations I am often…

  _____

- I am proud of being…

  _____

Once you have finished the sentences, just pause for a moment. If you are doing this exercise by yourself, you may want to write down why you feel these particular qualities came into your awareness. There is no need to be modest here. Quite the contrary! You can be as appreciative of yourself as you like.

If you are doing this exercise with someone else, then you may want to share with each other the qualities that came up and expand a bit on what these specific ones mean to you. Is there a story to tell? Take at least five minutes each. When you don't know what else to say, that's exactly when it becomes interesting. Then you'll get to see more of yourself.

For example

On the next page you will find the qualities that eldest daughters attributed to themselves during the Eldest Daughter Day. This is not an exclusive list by any means and you may find other positive qualities that suit you better. This list is just to help you get started.

| | |
|---|---|
| Able to handle a lot | Lively |
| Action oriented | Loyal |
| Ambitious | Loving |
| Analytical | Listener |
| Authentic | Mediator |
| Bright | Multifaceted |
| Caring | Open |
| Cheerful | Optimistic |
| Connector | Organizer |
| Communicator | Original |
| Conscientious | Passion |
| Content | Persistent |
| Creative | Positive |
| Down to earth | Powerful |
| Driven | Practical |
| Empathy | Pure |
| Enthusiastic | Relaxed |
| Firm | Reliable |
| Friendly | Silent enjoyment |
| Having an overview | Social |
| Helping hand | Solution oriented |
| Honest | Spontaneous |
| Humour | Stable |
| Idealistic | Stamina |
| Independent | Strong |
| Innovator | Sunny |
| Incorruptible | Trustworthy |
| Joyful | Understanding |
| Large perspective | Well-balanced |
| Lifesaver | |

## Step 2

Now the focus is on the flip-side. Just as we all do, you have your weaknesses and pitfalls. Time to look at those now. Take a new sheet of paper, Post-its of a different colour or cards that you mark on one side with a big minus sign. Direct your attention to the areas of yourself that you're not so well-pleased with. Again, allow some time for the three sentences to land, don't think too long and write down quickly whatever comes up. Be honest, even when you might feel a sense of shame for the quality you write down. Don't water it down; just give a sincere reply. Again you may find inspiration in the list we generated during the Eldest Daughter Day, in 'For example' on the next page.

These are the sentences to finish:

- A quality of mine that I find irritating is being...

———————————————————————————————————

- Others tend to say that at times I am...

———————————————————————————————————

- In difficult situations I am inclined to be...

———————————————————————————————————

If you do this exercise on your own, spend a few moments reflecting on why these particular pitfalls came into your awareness. There is nothing to be ashamed of. Every human being, each eldest daughter has sides that we consider less desirable. However, whenever we shed light on our shadow aspects, something might shift. This is especially the case when you can keep your heart open. No one is perfect and you don't need to be either.

When you do this exercise in the company of others, you may want to share your findings. Agree on this being confidential information that will not leave the room. None of you will discuss what you are sharing with a third party. Thus you create a safe space for one another. Also, it doesn't necessarily need to be a heavy and serious conversation when you disclose why you wrote down the qualities you did. There is no need to feel bad about yourself or start to feel down when you relate the story behind this — see if you can tell the story without overly identifying with it. Take at least five minutes each and don't interrupt but listen attentively, especially when the other person seems at a loss as to what to say. In moments like that, your open heart may help someone dig a bit deeper.

## For example

Below you will find the negative qualities that eldest daughters said they had during the Eldest Daughter Day. Again, this is not an exclusive list by any means and you might not recognize or understand a number of them. We're all different in our fallibility. This list is not meant to cajole you into unsuspected vices but to show what weak points others identified in themselves. By scanning through them you might find that different words to describe your own lesser qualities pop into your mind.

| | |
|---|---|
| Agitated | Dissatisfied |
| Always bearing others in mind | Distant |
| Always wanting to take care of | Dominant |
|    others | Emotional |
| Angry | Evasive |
| Apathy | Expecting too much from others |
| Apt to go into attack first | Fanatical |
| Being first to spring into action | Feeling discouraged |
| Being understanding for too | Feeling unappreciated |
|    long | Finding it hard to say 'no' |
| Big mouth | Grumpy |
| Bitchy | Heavy |
| Biting off more than I can chew | Hesitant |
| Bossy | Holding back |
| Careful | Ignore what I don't want to see |
| Chaotic | Impatient |
| Contrary | Impulsive |
| Control freak | Indirect (not saying what I |
| Crabby |    mean) |
| Critical | Insecure |
| Cynical | Intolerant |

| | |
|---|---|
| Irritable | Reserved |
| Jealous | Responsible for all and sundry |
| Judgemental | Rigid |
| Keeping an eye on everything | Self-criticism |
| Know-it-all | Self-destructive |
| Light-footed | Self-sacrificing |
| Meddlesome | Sense of guilt |
| Messy | Serious |
| Modest | Severe |
| Nagging | Stand outside of myself |
| Naive | Strict |
| Never good enough syndrome | Stubborn |
| Not truly saying what I mean | Taking a back seat |
| Obstinate | Taking on responsibility too |
| Panicky | easily |
| Perfectionist | Too direct (not count to ten) |
| Ponderous | Too eager to carry the load |
| Preoccupied | Too fast on my feet |
| Principled | Undiplomatic |
| Procrastinating | Uptight |
| Rational | Wanting to do too much |
| Refuse to give up | Wanting to get the last word in |
| Refuse to let go | Wanting to organize everyone |

## Step 3

Now that you have mapped your strong and weaker points, you may want to look at them at a deeper level using these questions as a guideline:

- What did you notice?
- What came as a surprise?
- What made you smile?
- What had you expected in the first place?

Again you may want to answer these questions by quietly allowing impressions, feelings, memories and thoughts to arise from within you. If you do the exercise with others, you may want to take some time for yourself first before you share – still with the agreement that what is being said stays within the four walls of the room.

You could compare your qualities to the ones from the list compiled during the Eldest Daughter Day. This will help to show that you are not alone. Throughout this book you will have read that eldest daughters, broadly speaking, share a number of characteristics. We all have our own story to tell too, but, sharing the position of the female firstborn, we also may have more in common than you would have thought.

# Bibliography

W e're happy to share with you the books that we read and found interesting, useful and entertaining. We've listed them in order of the year of their publication, and given a brief description.

## Selected (auto)biographies
## by eldest daughters

### *Thrive (2014)*, **Arianna Huffington**
President and editor-in-chief of the Huffington Post Media Group, one of the fastest growing media companies in the world, Arianna Huffington is extraordinarily successful by any measure. Yet, here she concludes that the pursuit of money and power has led to an erosion in the quality of relationships and family life. An eldest daughter with a sister who is also her best friend and a mother of two daughters herself, she draws on the latest scientific research to point the way to a balanced life.

### *Yesterday, Today, Tomorrow: My life (2014)*, **Sophia Loren**
One of last century's leading movie stars, known for her striking beauty and dramatic roles, Sophia Loren was born in a poor neighbourhood in Naples, Italy in 1934. She became an icon. In her autobiography she shares how she endured poverty and near starvation in her grandparents' house with her single mother and younger sister. Her mother saw the potential of her eldest daughter and entered her in a beauty pageant. Coming in first launched her memorable career, which would span six decades. Wise and candid, this eldest daughter portrays herself as a serious, hard-working woman who never gives up.

*Lean In (2013),* **Sheryl Sandberg**
Women need to sit at the table and not hover in the background, according to Sheryl Sandberg, chief operating officer of Facebook and one of *Fortune* magazine's Most Powerful Women in Business. She wants other women to join her at the top and she has done her research on what makes women hold back while men stride forth. An eldest of three, she is not afraid to share stories of her own inner turmoil while making her career on the fast track.

*I Am Malala (2013),* **Malala Yousafzai with Christina Lamb**
Entering the school founded by her father is magical to Malala: she can cast off her headscarf, drink in knowledge and be top of her class. Until that fateful day in 2012, when the Taliban shot her three times in the head for campaigning for girls' education. One bullet was removed in her native Pakistan before she was flown to the UK for further treatment. Malala's mission is to demand decisive action to educate girls and empower them to change their lives and communities.

*Dot Complicated (2013),* **Randi Zuckerberg**
A multifaceted go-getter, Randi Zuckerberg wrote a book about her six years as head of marketing at Facebook. Advocating a healthy tech–life balance, she is now a worldwide speaker on social media and marketing while also running her own boutique marketing firm and production company. Her book gives an insider's view on the start and the future of how Silicon techies change our lives. Between the lines it also gives an insider's view of her struggle to become a person in her own right and not just Mark Zuckerberg's older sister.

*Battle Hymn of the Tiger Mother (2011),* **Amy Chua**
'Nothing is fun until you are good at it.' The Yale Law School professor's clever account of how she raised her two daughters, Sophia and Lulu, to be brilliant at everything came as a shock to many. Amy Chua, eldest of four sisters, portrays Western parents as softies who would rather give in

to their children than insist they come home with straight As and practise the violin for two hours before and after school. A Chinese mother keeps driving her children. Sophia, the eldest, does as she is told; second-born Lulu, however…

### *Nothing Holds Back the Night (2011)*, Delphine de Vigan

In this moving autobiographical novel, French author Delphine de Vigan traces back the life of her mother, a former child model from a bohemian family. Doing so, she finds out more about herself as the eldest of two daughters from a broken family. Her first novel, also autobiographical, about overcoming anorexia, deserves to be translated into English too; it portrays the desperate attempts of an eldest daughter to take responsibility for her estranged parents and her younger sister.

### *My Father's Daughter (2011)*, Gwyneth Paltrow

Her father Bruce was the first love of her life. He loved to cook and the American Academy Award-winning actress and style icon learned his tastes and his skills while helping him in the kitchen as a young girl. Now she involves her own children in cooking healthy food for those who mean most to them. While not a classic autobiography, this luscious collection of organic, mouthwatering family recipes also reads as a testimony to the bond a father and daughter can enjoy.

### *Madam Secretary (2003)*, Madeleine Albright

It seemed a most unimaginable honour to be able to be of assistance to Bill Clinton in exerting American influence on the changing world. Madeleine Albright was born in Czechoslovakia. Her parents fled to London when she was two, returned home after the Second World War, then finally emigrated to the United States. For Albright democracy was at the heart of her time in public office. She talks about what she could and could not achieve, how proud she is of her efforts and how hard it was to go back to 'just' being a mother, grandmother, eldest sister and friend.

*Memoirs of a Dutiful Daughter (1958),* **Simone de Beauvoir**
If you want to know what life was like half a century ago, read the memoirs of French thinker and writer Simone de Beauvoir. She seems to remember every little detail of her early life when she was proud to be the eldest, to be first. She defied the social conventions of her time, with her love life and her feminism.

*Erstgeborene* **(2000), Jirina Prekop**
The books of the controversial, originally Czech psychologist who made her career in Germany have not been translated into English. In this one, titled "Firstborn" in German, Prekop describes how she considered herself a second-rate child in comparison with her beautiful, brilliant eldest sister. Only when she was in her seventies did she discover her eldest sister had had the opposite impression.

## Children's books

*The Baby Swap (2013),* **Jan Ormerod (with pictures by Andrew Joyner)**
A lovely picture book that tells the story of the confusion a firstborn girl experiences at the crucial moment that a second child is born. In this sweet story on jealousy and love, eldest daughter Caroline Crocodile is not thrilled with her baby brother. Mama Crocodile keeps saying how gorgeous he is. When Caroline is asked to watch him for a while, she ventures into a baby shop to swap him…

*My Firstborn, There's No One Like You (2004),* **Dr Kevin Leman & Kevin Leman II**
The firstborn cub would like to know if her mother loves her best. Mama Bear pulls her eldest onto her lap and tells her the story of her young life. Of course, the mother fell in love with her child the moment she was born. There is no one like her special firstborn – but her three cubs all make her heart smile. A father-and-son production by the internationally known psychologist, humourist and bestseller author and his youngest cub Kevin, who drew

the illustrations. This is one in a series of three for each child in the birth order: firstborn, middle and youngest cub – and each one is oh, so different.

## Selected professional publications

*'Why First-Born Kids Do Better In School' (2015)*, V. Joseph Hotz
Time and again, research shows that firstborn children are better at a lot of things than their younger siblings. So much so that even economists like professor Hotz, who specializes in labour economics, economic demography and economics of the family, takes an interest. One of his findings is that children's school performance declines with birth order, as does the stringency of parents' disciplinary restrictions. The higher intelligence of firstborns he attributes to the parents' strategy of strict disciplining with their first child in the hope of inducing preferred school effort levels among their later-borns.

*http://www.slate.com/articles/double_x/doublex/2013/10/birth_order_ and_school_performance_first_borns_do_better_in_school_because.html*

*'The Science of Superiority: Why The Firstborn Child Is The Smartest One' (2015)*, John Haltiwanger
Entertaining piece full of links to studies and articles by the senior politics writer at Elite Daily, the popular Facebook page. From the perspective of a younger child, he grumbles at firstborns' success and the inevitable praise lavished on them while the younger sibling is sitting in the corner wearing their hand-me-downs and wondering where it all went wrong. Haltiwanger shows that all is not lost for outgoing, competitive, flexible, diplomatic and decidedly social middle children or persistent, charming and affectionate last-borns.

*http://elitedaily.com/life/culture/firstborn-children-are- more-intelligent/874899/* (Jan 5 2015)

*Do Fathers Matter? (2014)*, Paul Raeburn
Science reporter and father of five, Paul Raeburn, wondered how important fathers really are in the lives of their children. He also wanted to know if he was getting things right. Extensive research led to his conclusion that the

impact of fathers on the lives of their children cannot be overestimated. The essence of fatherhood to him is to help children become happy and healthy adults.

### 'Sibling Configurations, Educational Aspiration and Attainment' (2014), Feifei Bu

Lead researcher at the University of Essex, Feifei Bu, used sibling data drawn from over 3,500 British children to compare aspirations and achievements. Her study confirms earlier findings: eldest children often have higher aspirations and attain higher levels of education as a result of this. She also flags the parental investment that peaks with the first child and diminishes over time. Bu has a personal interest in studying sibling structures: she is an eldest daughter herself; that's why she is doing a PhD. Her findings that, especially, eldest daughters excel were picked up by media worldwide.

> *https://www.iser.essex.ac.uk/publications/working-papers/iser/*
> *2014-11.pdf*

### Daring Greatly (2012), Brené Brown

Vulnerability is not a sign of weakness but the path to a fulfilling life. This world-famous research professor at the University of Houston, Texas is the eldest of four and has an eldest daughter herself. Using the method of Grounded Theory, she has spoken to thousands of people across the United States. Finding the underlying patterns within these interviews she shows why we are so afraid to be vulnerable and what happens when you find the courage to step forth, as she did when she gave her first TED Talk on the subject in 2010, which now ranks in the top ten most popular talks.

### Birth Order (2011), Linda Blair

An accessible book by an American eldest daughter who worked as a clinical psychologist in England for thirty years. She appeared regularly on radio and television shows. Blair gives a list of characteristics typical of each of the four main birth-order positions – first, middle, youngest and single children.

This makes for an entertaining read out loud to your family or friends, as the recognition factor will be high. It must be noted that it seems to us she has rewritten Lucille Forer's 1969 book all over again, although she does not mention this author in the references.

### *The Sibling Effect (2011),* Jeffrey Kluger

After writing a couple of cover stories on the burgeoning field of sibling research for *Time* magazine, journalist Jeffrey Kluger spent three years talking to the best researchers in the field. He interlaces his findings with a personal account of his own experiences of the birth order wars with his brothers, the divorce of his parents and the step-siblings and half-siblings who came with remarriage. An intelligent and moving book, especially for men who want to know more of what the bonds between brothers and sisters reveal about us.

### *The Secret Power of Middle Children (2011),* Catherine Salmon and Katrin Schumann

Typically, middle children feel undervalued because of being, well, in the middle. Combining research in evolutionary biology, psychology and sociology with real-life stories, psychologist Catherine Salmon, PhD, and journalist Katrin Schumann show how middle children cultivate a spirit of independence. They are excellent negotiators and mediators; they know how to bridge a gap. With families shrinking in size, middle children are becoming an increasingly rare species. The authors show us what a loss that is.

### *The Gifts of Imperfection (2010),* Brené Brown

Being connected is what life is all about. However, to be able to feel connected we need to show ourselves as we are, accept our imperfection and muster the courage to be authentic. In this beautiful book, filled with stories about her own fear of rejection, Brené Brown shows how hard – and how rewarding – it is to let go of who you think you ought to be and embrace your perfect imperfection.

*The Idle Parent (2009)*, **Tom Hodgkinson**
Why all the fuss about parenting, this well-known British writer wanted to know. Children who have too much done for them cannot do things for themselves. Doing less for your children will make them self-reliant, is at the core not only of his advice but also of his daily practice. In 1993, he and a friend started the magazine the *Idler*, a yearly British magazine devoted to enjoying things as they come rather than toiling for an imagined better future. Parenting should certainly not be hard work, according to Hodgkinson in his witty account of putting theory into practice.

*Strangers in a Strange Lab (2009)*, **William Ickes**
Distinguished professor of psychology at the University of Texas, William Ickes has studied personality influences on initial interactions for thirty years. How good are we at knowing what goes on inside someone else's mind? What makes us better or worse at gauging this? Based on his studies, done in dyads, he makes statements on the impact of your birth position on your love life: the more you resemble one another, the better.

*You Were Always Mom's Favorite! (2009)*, **Deborah Tannen**
You love your sister to pieces *and* she can drive you nuts. Professor of linguistics at Georgetown University Deborah Tannen endeavours to understand and explain how the language of conversation reflects – and affects – relationships. She conducted conversations with over one hundred women on their relationship with their sisters. Highlighting the stories that women tell about their intense, heartbreaking, frustrating and rewarding sisterly experiences, Tannen shows how inextricably linked sisters are. A youngest herself, her own two sisters have been a cherished part of her life.

*The Birth Order Book of Love (2008)*, **William Cane**
As a professor of English for years Cane, an eldest son, tested on colleagues and students Walter Toman's findings that the best partnerships in love mirror the roles people played growing up in their family. So: an eldest sister of

brothers is best matched with a youngest brother of elder sisters. Nowadays he lectures on this subject all over the United States while also being a couples' counsellor. After thirty-eight years of study and observation, he can assure us that birth order is much more than a scientific curiosity. While not being perfect, it is in his view the most reliable way to find out about your personality and romantic compatibility.

*The F1rstborn Advantage (2008),* **Kevin Leman**
'As new, excited parents, we made all the mistakes. Yes, we admit we practiced on you. You, our firstborn, were our guinea pig,' writes psychologist, humourist and bestselling author Dr Kevin Leman in the dedication of this book to his daughter Holly. In his view there is more to birth order than meets the eye; you can be an eighth-born child and have a firstborn personality. In this entertaining book he puts the pieces of the puzzle together.

*'Sibling Relations and Their Impact on Children's Development' (2006),* **Nina Howe, PhD and Holly Recchia, MA**
A short, interesting paper by two researchers at the Centre for Research in Human Development, Concordia University, Canada. Approximately eighty per cent of Western children have at least one sibling and the sibling relationship is likely to last longer than any other relationship in one's lifetime, and be one of the most intimate. In the real-life lab of growing up together, siblings provide each other with an important context for understanding other people's minds, emotions, thoughts, intentions and beliefs.
    http://www.enfant-encyclopedie.com/pages/PDF/
    Howe-RecchiaANGxp.pdf

*Constructing Grounded Theory (2006),* **Kathy Charmaz**
To allow the theory to arise from the analysis of systematically collected data – that is the basis of this research method, developed in 1967 by two social scientists. From interviews, conversations and research studies you collect a wealth of data that you separate, sort and synthesize. You then write pre-

liminary analytic notes that form the basis of your theory that in this way is a rendition of life itself. We conducted our research in this way and are grateful to Kathy Charmaz for this practical guide.

*Mother–Daughter Wisdom (2005),* **Christiane Northrup**

After being a practising physician for twenty-five years, gynaecologist Dr Christiane Northrup gained international fame with her empowering talks and books. An expert on women's health and wellness at any age, she addresses vitality in mind, body, emotions and spirit. A mother of two grown-up daughters, she wanted to show how deeply the relationship between mother and daughters impacts the well-being of women. In this book, based on her own experiences as a mother and physician, she offers practical, medical, spiritual and personal advice.

*Why First-Borns Rule the World and Last-Borns Want to Change it (2003),* **Michael Grose**

The teacher turned author and counsellor in the field of education distinguishes three types of firstborns: the leader of the pack, the shepherd (or second mother/father) and the hard driver (or high-octane superwoman/man). This well-written book is full of practical advice for parents who, of course, come with the characteristics of their own position in the birth order. Grose is a clear admirer of Frank Sulloway, who in turn is inspired by the views and theories of Charles Darwin.

*What a Difference a Daddy Makes (2000),* **Dr Kevin Leman**

According to this psychologist and master communicator, being consistent is the most important ingredient of a healthy father–daughter relationship. The reason is that consistency builds a foundation of trust, and this trust then forms the basis of the kinds of relationships your daughter will form with men throughout her life. A father to four daughters himself, Leman interweaves scientific findings on effective fathering with funny and moving stories about his own parenting. His primary recommendation to fathers: spend a lot of time with your daughters, be involved and set her free.

### Birth Order Blues (1999), Meri Wallace

As this New York psychotherapist listened to parents talk about their family problems, she came to see that birth order issues were often at the bottom of many sibling battles and difficult parent–child relationships. Through telling the stories of clients from her private practice, she shows the family situations viewed from their individual perspectives. Describing the typical struggles of oldest, middle and youngest children, she offers ways to work with each child in the birth order.

### Love's Hidden Symmetry (1998), Bert Hellinger with Gunthard Weber and Hunter Beaumont

Hellinger is the innovative therapist who introduced systemic work with family constellations. He is also an amazing storyteller. This book is a lively blend of narrative, storytelling and transcripts of sessions on the central theme of how to make love work in relationships.

### Separate lives: Why Siblings Are So Different (1990), Judy Dunn and Robert Plomin

The two professors of human development at Pennsylvania State University make a single, simple point: persons growing up in the same family differ very much from one another in personality, talents, emotional security, confidence and style. Presenting evidence from systematic research, they illustrate their points with stories of writers, their families and biographers. DNA makes siblings share traits; everything else makes the difference.

### Birth Order & You (1990), Dr Ronald Richardson and Lois A. Richardson

Between each birth the family undergoes a reshaping, so one could argue that each child is born to different parents in a different setting. This couple base their book on the question 'Why am I like this?' on the findings of psychologist Walter Toman. For their own observations they draw on his long years as a marriage counsellor and family therapist. Their hope is that learning more about the usual characteristics for their sex and birth order will help people understand and accept themselves.

*'The beginnings of social understanding' (1988),* **Judy Dunn**
Sitting in kitchens and living rooms, this professor of human development observed the interactions between eldest children, their parents and their siblings. One of the remarkable findings of her 'Cambridge' study within the family context is that children early in their second year already show a clear practical grasp of how to annoy, comfort, tease or support an other child, much earlier than was commonly thought.

*The Birth Order Book (1985),* **Dr Kevin Leman**
Have you ever wondered why you are so different from your siblings? Why you pick the friends you do, the lovers? This popular and forever positive psychologist can answer all those questions, having studied the effects of birth order for over thirty years. Birth order makes sense if you want to know why you are the way you are, according to Leman, and he can even explain the exceptions to the birth order rules. A book full of advice, such as: 'Sensitive perfectionists need to do nice things for themselves.'

*Family Ties That Bind (1984),* **Dr Ronald W. Richardson**
Most of us leave our family home physically one day but we rarely leave it emotionally. Even if we put an ocean between ourselves and our family, or never return home again, we will continue to re-enact the dynamics of our original family in any new family that we establish, even if the context is completely different. Family therapist Richardson describes the tension between wanting to be the same and different from the rest of your family well and with a kind tone, in this self-help book.

*Born To Rebel (1977),* **Frank J. Sulloway**
Treading in the footsteps of Charles Darwin, this American psychologist sees families as ecosystems in which siblings compete for parental favour by choosing a specific niche. Each child tries to be different. Thus, each child enhances their own unique qualities, with the eldest having first choice. Sulloway combed through thousands of biographies in politics, science and religion.

His conclusion: firstborns are more likely to identify with authority while their younger siblings are predisposed to rise against it. Given the nature of his research his often-cited work is predominantly based on the lives of historic men.

### *The Managerial Woman (1976),* Margaret Hennig and Anne Jardim

In 1973, these Harvard Business School-educated consultants started to interview women in management positions about how they got ahead. This gave a consistent picture of women who are very good at what they do, and very bad at estimating what it takes to make it to the top. A groundbreaking book in its time.

### *The Female Eunuch (1970),* Germaine Greer

With her humour, boldness and wit, Australian-born feminist, and eldest daughter, Greer took the world by storm stating that a revolution was needed to reconnect women with their sexuality. Women should get to know, respect, revere and enjoy their own bodies again instead of living up to the stereotype set by the consumer society.

### *Birth Order and Life Roles (1969),* Lucille K. Forer

'I was the first child of my parents,' clinical psychologist Forer writes in her introduction. 'I was followed by a brother and a sister and then, after a long period of time, by another brother. While these facts were not of great importance to the world in general, they seemed very important to me.' Combining research in psychological literature with her clinical observations of the effect of sibling relationships, Forer presents evidence for consistent differences especially between firstborn and later-born children. A lovely, albeit a bit outdated book.

### *Family Constellation (1961),* Walter Toman

Over the course of ten years clinical psychologist Toman studied four hundred people, their sibling positions, those of their parents, grandparents (if possible) and their children. His research led him to conclude that people of the same sex and the same position in the birth order show great similarities in attitude towards authority, property, work, religion and philosophy. He shows how the way you relate to your siblings and your parents impacts your future relationships. His examples show how much has changed in the past half-century and are a little dated. The underlying principles of how we act on the basis of our birth order, however, remain fascinating.

### *Brothers and Sisters (1958),* Karl König
This book on the effects of the order of birth in the family by this Austrian paediatrician became a classic. König distinguishes three basic patterns: the firstborn strives to conquer the world; the second attempts to live in harmony with the world; the third is given to avoiding direct confrontation with the world. The fourth child resembles the first again and so on. This is an interesting and important little book from an anthroposophical perspective.

### *The Eldest Child (1957),* Edith Neisser
The position of the eldest poses questions that go wide and run deep. Neisser wrote this book, which is grounded in sound principles of child psychology, because of concerns being expressed by parents, teachers, social workers and doctors at the time about the special problems an eldest must work out. The position of an eldest is, of course, different now than in her day. Yet, these cases from over half a century ago still speak to the unique inner pressures that shape an eldest's feelings about parents, siblings and the wider family.

### *The Education of Children (1930),* Alfred Adler
His ideas on raising children come across as old-fashioned now, but the Austrian psychiatrist was the first to state that who you become relates to a large extent to your place within the family. He believed that every child feels inferior. In striving for superiority and success to compensate for this uncomfortable feeling, eldest, middle, youngest and only children develop along the same lines, was his observation.

# Test your insight into the influence of birth order

Even if you have never before given the subject any thought, almost everyone turns out to be quite good at guessing the place someone occupies in the birth order of their family. Here's a test to gauge your insight into whether you are dealing with an only, eldest, middle or youngest child. In these descriptions do you see an eldest daughter, a middle one, a youngest or an only child?

1.  Even as a child my sister could get away with anything. She has this gift of making friends wherever she goes. Her job? What do you think? She is a star in sales, of course.

2.  She feels responsible for everybody. Whoever knocks on her door finds a listening ear. I have no clue where she finds the time to do as much as she does. Yet still she thinks she doesn't do enough.

3.  My sister is a terrific mediator. She gets people to speak to one another who have avoided each other for years.

4.  It isn't always easy to have her as a sister. She sets a high standard and she seems to have a perfect life, but for others it is often difficult to find out how she really feels.

5.  I get along better with older people than I do with my peers. That's just how it is. Some people think I am arrogant or self-centred. Actually, I'm not.

6.  My girlfriend is a bit of a maverick. A rebel who likes to forge her own way. She has a lot of friends but her independence comes first.

7.  I don't know why people worry so much. I am not at all self-sufficient but there is always someone around who can help me and I have no qualms about asking.

8.  My sister has always been a high achiever. She works for a TV show. Leave it to her to get hold of the perfect guest and give the presenter all the facts.

# Acknowledgements

The idea for this book was born when our Dutch publisher Daniël Doornink shared a story about his eldest daughter in which we could instantly identify patterns we knew intimately from our own lives. We are immensely grateful for how he as a youngest son supported our eldest-daughter investigations. We also have him to thank for taking the book to the Frankfurt Book Fair. Here, Krisztina Katjar gracefully invited us into a deeper conversation at the Findhorn Press stand, where Sabine Weeke saw the potential. We are grateful to her for being true to her hunch, and for the inspiring collaboration we have since enjoyed. Thank you, Thierry Bogliolo of Findhorn Press, for listening to this eldest daughter. You know how close Findhorn is to Lisette's heart so we are immensely happy to have landed on your list.

We could not have done our research without the invaluable contributions of the eldest daughters who helped us organize and hold the Eldest Daughter Day – thank you for your wisdom and skill, Lenneke Aalbers, Pamela van den Berg and Odette Kramps who formed the core team with us, and to Aike Borghuis, Kim Hagenaar, Anne-Floor Kok, Nani Lehnhausen, Judith Manshanden, Stephanie Schuitemaker, Manoesjka Snijders and Marion Witter for their enthusiasm to assist us on this memorable day. A deep bow of gratitude also to youngest sons Wim Lehnhausen and Dik van der Stroom of Amsterdam Studio's for doing the groundwork. And to all the eldest daughters who came and shared their life stories so freely.

We were fortunate to find an intelligent and insistent editor of the Dutch version in Aimée Warmerdam. The valuable comments of eldest daughters Saskia Otter and Chiquita van Teylingen Bakker had us make some necessary revisions, while Caroline de Gruyter's comments on the chapter on your own eldest daughter also proved crucial. For the English version Emily Eaves was a joy to work with, fast and reliable. Lucy McCarraher and Gill Emslie gave us valuable feedback that we have happily included. Then came whirlwind final copy-editor Jacqui Lewis – thank you for the ping-pong game of bouncing the text back and forth, better with each iteration. We would also like to acknowledge the contributions of Michael Hawkins with his keen eye as a proofreader and Damian Keenan with his fabulous design.

Both of us feel deep gratitude to our men, Jos van Merendonk and Wim Lehnhausen. We now know it is no accident that both of you are youngest sons. You have supported us through the thick and thin of this project of almost two years that has enriched our friendship as couples. Through this book we hope you'll understand us even better than before.

Most of all we are grateful to our parents, Miek and the late Albert Schuitemaker and Rie and the late Eep Enthoven, and of course our sisters and brothers – Albert, Aleid and Michiel for Lisette, and Albertien for Wies. We would never have become the eldest daughters we are without you.

# About the Authors

**WIES ENTHOVEN** (left) has long worked as a freelance journalist for leading Dutch newspapers and magazines. She wrote her first book on frightened heroes as she calls all those who through illness need to find the strength to face each day and change their lives. Currently, she mainly works as a writing coach for authors, individuals and people in business, also applying the proprioceptive writing method. She is the eldest daughter of an eldest daughter and has an eldest daughter herself.

**LISETTE SCHUITEMAKER** (right), eldest of four, founded and ran a communications agency that had many of the major Dutch companies as its clients. After selling her business, she obtained a BSc in Brennan Healing Science. This is her third book, the second one having been published in English under the title *Alight*. Apart from writing, she serves as chair of the Center for Human Emergence, the Netherlands and the Findhorn Foundation, Scotland.